SOCCER

MASTERING THE BASICS WITH THE PERSONALIZED SPORTS INSTRUCTION SYSTEM

David Carr
Ohio University

Michael Metzler
Georgia State University

Allyn and Bacon
Boston London Toronto Sydney Tokyo Singapore

VICE PRESIDENT	Paul A. Smith
Publisher	Joseph E. Burns
EDITORIAL ASSISTANT	Annemarie Kennedy
MARKETING MANAGER	Rick Muhr
EDITORIAL PRODUCTION SERVICE	Bernadine Richey Publishing Services
TEXT DESIGN AND COMPOSITION	Barbara Bert Silbert
MANUFACTURING BUYER	Julie McNeill
COVER ADMINISTRATOR	Brian Gogolin

Internet: www.abacon.com

ISBN: 0-205-32371-5

Printed in the United States of America

10 9 8 7 6 5 4 3 2 1   05 04 03 02 01 00

SOCCER

CONTENTS

PREFACE

INTRODUCTION TO PSIS SOCCER

Hello, and welcome to your **soccer class**! That's right, *your* soccer class. This personal workbook includes almost everything you will need to learn the game of soccer and become a proficient beginning-level player. Of course, your instructor will play an important part as you progress, but most of what you will need is contained in your Personal Workbook. Your soccer class will be taught this term using the **Personalized Sports Instruction System (PSIS)**, developed specifically for college basic instruction courses like the one in which you are enrolled. All of the materials in this workbook have been refined in field tests with many students like yourself, college men and women getting their first formal soccer instruction.

The key design feature of the PSIS is that it allows for individualized learning and progression through the course. Think back to other classes you have taken: some students learn faster than others. This is a fact in all learning situations. Depending on individual learning rate, some students become frustrated if the course goes too fast. Others become bored if the course goes too slowly. Either way, many students become disinterested, reducing their enjoyment of the course. For soccer, the most harmful result of frustration or boredom is that students are not given a proper chance to learn the game and to enjoy it as a regular part of their activity schedule. Whether you are a "bare beginner" or currently have some soccer experience, the PSIS design will allow you to progress **"as quickly as you can, or as slowly as you need."** Keep this little motto in mind as you become familiar with this workbook and progress through your soccer class this term.

Another point to keep in mind is that the PSIS is *achievement oriented*. That means the PSIS design is intended to help you learn the necessary skills, strategies, and rules for beginning soccer play. We guarantee you will be a better player at the end of your PSIS class than you are now!

As you will see, your improvement will come in a way that is different from most other courses you have taken. You will be asked to assume more responsibility for your own learning than ever before. Remember, all the instructional material is included in your Personal Workbook. It will be up to you to learn the contents of the workbook, become familiar with the PSIS system, attend class regularly, follow your instructor's class policies, and work diligently toward completing the course sequences. It has been our experience that college students enjoy taking a large role in their own learning and appreciate the individualized plan of the PSIS. We know that you will, too.

ADVANTAGES OF THE PSIS FOR YOU

1. **The PSIS reduces your dependence on the instructor.** Your Personal Workbook provides nearly all the information you will need to complete the course. All content, learning task, and managerial information is at your fingertips, not with the instructor. When you are ready for a new learning task, the individualized plan will allow you to proceed on your own.
2. **Individualized learning is emphasized.** The PSIS will allow you to learn soccer "as quickly as you can, or as slowly as you need." You will be able to remain in your own comfort zone while progressing through the course.
3. **You will have increased responsibility for your own learning.** As adult learners, college students can assume responsibility for much of their own learning. You can make decisions that have direct bearing on class attendance, practice routines, and achievement. The PSIS system shifts much of the responsibility and decision making directly to you and away from the instructor.
4. **Your access to the instructor will be increased whenever you need it.** Since PSIS instructors can spend much more time in class teaching students, it means that you will get more personal attention and quality instruction, *that is, if you need it.* If you do not require as much interaction with the instructor, it will not be forced on you as with group learning strategies.
5. **You can chart your own progress.** Your PSIS Soccer Personal Workbook includes a simple Personal Progress Chart to help you gauge your learning as you go through the course. This will help you to make decisions about your learning pace, projected grade, and how to use your class time most efficiently.

YOUR ROLE IN PSIS SOCCER

Your role in PSIS Soccer can be summarized easily: become familiar with and follow the Personal Workbook as an independent learning guide. You will not need to depend on the instructor for content and managerial information. But when the workbook is not sufficient or specific learning information is needed, you should be sure to *ASK FOR HELP*! Your Personal Workbook will provide nearly all the information needed to complete the course. So, if you can progress without the instructor's direction, the system is designed to let you. If you need help, the instructor will be free to provide it for you. Your instructor will show you a *help signal* for getting his or her attention in class. It might be a raised hand or a verbal call. Be sure you know this signal, and do not be shy about using it!

YOUR INSTRUCTOR'S ROLE IN PSIS SOCCER

Your instructor has the important role of *facilitator* in your PSIS soccer course. Your Personal Workbook will provide most of the content and management information you will need, providing your instructor more time to give students individual attention. There will be just one large-group demonstration throughout the entire course, and very little time will be spent organizing routine class "chores." Nearly all the instructor's time will be available to facilitate your learning on an individual basis.

Your instructor has the teaching experience and expertise to make the PSIS work as well as it was designed. The PSIS system allows the instructor to provide the maximum use of his or her expertise by *facilitating* the learning process for you.

SKILL AND KNOWLEDGE COURSE MODULES

Your PSIS soccer course contains a number of learning activities divided into a series of modules. There are two types of modules: **performance skill** and **soccer knowledge**. Performance skill modules focus on the major psychomotor performance patterns needed to play soccer. The soccer knowledge module contains information on basic game rules and soccer etiquette.

PSIS COURSE MANAGEMENT AND POLICIES

In this section you will learn some of the ways in which the PSIS approach can give you increased control over your own learning. Some course management and policies will come from your Personal Workbook. Others will be communicated to you by your instructor. Be sure that you are familiar with all course management routines and policies.

1. **Dressing for class.** You will need to have proper clothing and footwear in order to participate comfortably and safely in your soccer class. We suggest that you wear lightweight, loose-fitting clothes that will not restrict your range of motion (shorts, T-shirts, and the like). General-purpose court shoes or "cross training" shoes with white soles are recommended. Do not wear running shoes or shoes that will make marks on the floor. Specialized clothing and soccer shoes are not necessary. Be sure to ask your instructor about his or her policies regarding dressing for class.

2. **Equipment.** Your instructor will provide you with all the necessary equipment for class, and with the routines for distributing and collecting equipment each day.

3. **Depositing and distributing Personal Workbooks.** Your instructor will advise you on his or her policy regarding your workbook each day after class. We suggest that the instructor collect all student workbooks at the end of class and bring them to class the next day. Be sure that you know the exact policy to be used, since you cannot participate fully in class without your own workbook.

4. **Practice partners.** Some learning tasks will call for you to practice with one or more partners and be checked off by them. Any classmate can be your partner for most tasks. A few tasks will specify that all students in a drill be at the same place in the course learning sequence.

5. **Arriving to class.** Your instructor will inform you about specific routines for arriving to class and beginning each day. Generally, you should (1) arrive at or before the class starting time, (2) locate your own Personal Workbook, (3) complete your stretching and warm-up routine, (4) find a practice partner (if needed at that time), and (5) begin to practice the appropriate learning task. Note that you can begin as soon as you arrive. Except for the first day of instruction, the instructor will not wait to begin the class with all students together. *Arriving before class will allow you extra time to practice your soccer skills.*

6. **Self-checks, partner-checks, and instructor-checks.** Each learning task in PSIS soccer requires that your mastery be documented (checked off). Some tasks can be checked off by you, some must be checked off by a partner, and some by your instructor. Items are checked off by the appropriate person initialing and dating the designated area after each checked

task in your Personal Workbook. Instructor-checked tasks will require that you practice for a period of time prior to attempting mastery and being checked off. When you are ready, indicated by a series of successful trial blocks, signal the instructor and ask him or her to observe you. If you do not reach the stated criterion, you can return for more practice and signal for the instructor again at a later time. *There is no penalty for not making a mastery criterion. You can try as many times as it takes to be successful.* You may find it helpful to alert the instructor at the beginning of a class in which you anticipate needing his or her observation and checking. The instructor will then be on the lookout for your signal.

7. **Grading.** Your course instructor will inform you about the grading system and related policies to be used in your PSIS soccer class. Be sure you are aware of the specific requirements and procedures for determining your grade.

USING YOUR TIME EFFECTIVELY

Your PSIS soccer course is made up of a series of predetermined learning tasks grouped into twelve modules. Your course will have a set number of class days with a set class length. It is important for you to know your own learning pace and to make steady progress toward completing all course requirements. Therefore, you will need to learn how to best use your time in class and to accurately project completion of PSIS soccer before the end of the term. Here are some helpful tips for managing your time.

1. Arrive to class early and begin right away. No signal will be given by the instructor for class to begin.
2. Stay for the entire class period. Do not get into a habit of leaving early.
3. Learn the PSIS course management system right away. The quicker you understand how it works, the sooner you can start using it to your advantage.
4. Do not hesitate to ask the instructor for assistance. Learn and use the class help signal to get the instructor's attention.
5. If there is not enough time to complete a new task in a class, at least *start* it. This will save time the next day.
6. When you are close to finishing a task at the end of a class, try to stay a few minutes late to complete it. This avoids repetitious setup time the next day and the possible loss of your learning momentum.
7. When a practice partner is needed, pair up with the first person you can find, rather than waiting for a certain person. (This is good way to get to know more of your classmates!)
8. Alert the instructor prior to instructor-checked criterion tasks so that he or she will be available when you need observation and a check-off.

PSIS SOCCER LEARNING MODULES

This section will describe how the PSIS course learning modules are designed. It is important that you know how the PSIS works so that you can take advantage of its individualized learning features. The course learning content is included in two kinds of learning modules: **performance skill** and **soccer knowledge**.

Each *performance skill* module will include the following:

1. A written **introduction** to the skill
2. An **instructor demonstration** of the proper skill techniques
3. Text and photographs that explain the **components** or **phases** of each skill
4. Photographs that highlight the key **performance cues** (these same cues will be presented by the instructor in his or her demonstration).
5. Simple **comprehension tasks** and **readiness drills** to develop initial skill patterns
6. An **error analysis** and **correction section** for self-analyzing common mistakes
7. **Learning tips** for increased proficiency
8. A series of several **criterion tasks** for practicing and demonstrating your skill mastery
9. One or more **challenge tasks** for developing tactical applications of skills in modified competitive situations
10. A **Personal Recording Form** for selected tasks, used to record successful practice trials

The *soccer knowledge* module will include:

1. A **reading** on the basic rules of soccer and soccer game strategy
2. A **knowledge quiz** to test your understanding of the rules and strategy

CHARTING YOUR PROGRESS

The last page of your PSIS soccer workbook includes your **Personal Progress Chart**. Your instructor will show you how to correctly label the chart, and the rest is very simple. At the end of each week in the course, put an x above that date, and across from the last task you completed. As the weeks go by, you will begin to see how your individual learning pace projects your successful completion of all course learning modules.

This introductory section, combined with additional information from your instructor, will allow you to use the PSIS soccer workbook to your full advantage and to learning soccer at your own pace, with highly individualized attention from your instructor. Because PSIS soccer is a complete system for learning the game, it might take you a little time to become familiar with this approach. However, remember that your instructor is there to help when you have questions about the system and when you need individual attention for learning. Now that you know about the PSIS soccer system, you are probably anxious to get started. We hope you enjoy learning soccer with the PSIS approach and that you will become an avid player of this lifelong game. READY...SET...GO!!

MODULE 1

WARM-UP AND STRETCHING FOR SOCCER

INTRODUCTION

Soccer is played primarily with the feet, but in doing so all parts of the body are utilized. It is be important to help prepare the entire body for the rigors of playing soccer. There is constant turning, twisting, and stretching of the body during play. It is be important to combine initial body movement (running with the ball) with stretching of major muscle groups. Warm-up actually begins with increasing blood flow throughout the body by elevating your heart rate. Once this has occurred over the course of 3 to 5 minutes, stretching of the major muscle groups should begin.

Flexibility refers to the ability of the muscles, tendons, and ligaments around a joint to move while providing support and allowing the joint to move smoothly through its entire range of motion. Increased flexibility means more supple muscles, which reduces the risk of injury to the muscle when the limb is moved suddenly. Flexibility can be enhanced through an effective warm-up and stretching regimen.

A static method of stretching is common in preparation for sports participation and is useful in preparation for playing soccer. Static stretching should only occur after the body has been warmed through light activity. Running laps is not recommended. Dribbling the soccer ball in a restricted space is a perfect way to combine skill development, decision making, and warming the body for more rigorous play. A 3 to 5 minute dribbling program at the beginning of each class can help prepare the body for static stretching, which should be done with muscles that have been warmed. Static stretching with warm muscles has been shown to be a very effective method, especially when done slowly and carefully. A key thing to remember when stretching is *do not bounce*. Bouncing while stretching can cause muscle injury. By utilizing an effective warm-up and stretch program before and after activity, flexibility can be enhanced. The stretching of muscles around joints before and after vigorous movement improves blood flow and can help reduce postexercise soreness. Your course instructor should supervise your warm-up period to be sure the stretches are performed correctly and that you are ready to play soccer.

PERFORMANCE CUES

1. **Warm-up.** Increase the heart rate and flow of blood to muscles prior to stretching. Engage in light activity for 3 to 5 minutes prior to stretching. Dribbling a soccer ball in a restricted space is recommended because it presents an opportunity to work on skill development and decision making prior to more intense physical play.

2. **Do not bounce.** Move into each stretching position slowly and easily. Stretch the muscle until tension is felt and then hold your position for 15 seconds. This will allow the muscle to become more elastic. Bouncing can cause damage to the muscle.

3. **Hold the stretch.** This allows the muscle to accommodate to the rigors of strenuous exercise, it is important to allow the muscle to adapt to the stress of the stretching process. It is important to hold each stretch for a minimum of 15 seconds.

4. **Target zone.** You should not feel pain while stretching a muscle. The target zone is a point where there is maximum tension in the muscle but there is no pain. Stretching at a level below the target zone will not allow for complete stretching of the muscle, whereas stretching above the target zone increases the risk of injury.

5. **Breathing.** Do not hold your breath while stretching. Breathing should be normal and rhythmical.

6. **Postexercise stretching (cool down).** Stretching after the conclusion of strenuous exercise helps the body recover and helps reduce muscle soreness.

INSTRUCTOR DEMONSTRATION

Your course instructor will demonstrate each of the recommended stretching exercise for soccer. Observe each demonstration carefully, making note of the performance cues that follow.

Lower Back and Hamstring Stretch 1. With your feet slightly wider than shoulder width apart and the body bend forward at the waist, reach through your legs in the center and hold the stretch for at least 15 seconds. You should feel tension in your hamstrings. Legs should be straight but not locked. Refer to Photo 1.1. Repeat this stretch 3 times.

Photo 1.1
Lower back and hamstring stretch 1

Photo 1.2
Lower back and hamstring stretch 2

Lower Back and Hamstring Stretch 2. While standing upright, cross one leg over the other leg at the ankle. Bend at the waist keeping legs straight but not locked at the knee. Reach to the toes or ground immediately in front of the toes and hold for 15 seconds. Refer to Photo 1.2. Repeat 3 times and then switch legs.

Photo 1.3
Quadriceps stretch 1

Quadriceps (Thigh) Stretch 1. Stand on one foot and grab the other ankle with the hand opposite the leg you are stretching. Get your balance (use a partner to steady yourself) and pull the ankle toward your buttocks and hold for 15 seconds. Your heel should be close to your buttocks and you should feel tension in your quadriceps muscle. Refer to Photo 1.3. Repeat at least 3times for each leg.

Photo 1.4
Quadriceps stretch 2

Quadriceps (Thigh) Stretch 2. Gently lunge forward on one foot to a position that puts the quadriceps muscle parallel to the ground. The back leg should be extended behind you with the weight supported on the toe. The knee of the back leg should be about 4 to 6 inches off the ground. You should feel tension in the quadriceps muscle of the back leg and some tension in both the quadriceps and hamstring muscles of the leg that is in the forward or lunge position. Refer to Photo 1.4. Hold for 15 seconds and change legs. Repeat 3 times for each leg.

Photo 1.5
Overhead stretch

Overhead Stretch. Stand with feet approximately shoulder-width apart, place one hand on the lower quadriceps muscle, and raise the other hand up against the ear at the side of the head. Lean to the side opposite the raised arm and slide the other hand down the side of the leg until there is tension in the shoulder, rib cage, and abdomen. Refer to Photo 1.5. Hold this stretch for 15 seconds and then stretch in the opposite direction. Repeat 2 more times on each side.

Photo 1.6
Trunk twist stretch

Trunk Twist Stretch. Stand with feet approximately shoulder-width apart and turn sideways at the waist until tension is felt in the abdomen, shoulders, and lower back. Extend the lead arm (in the direction you twist) straight out and hold the trail arm tight across the chest. Do not twist back and forth. Refer to Photos 1.6A and B. Hold this stretch for 15 seconds and then twist in the opposite direction. Repeat 2 more times in each direction.

CRITERION TASK FOR STRETCHING

Partner-Checked

Pair up with another person in the class. In turn, have one partner perform stretch while the other observes looking for proper technique. Switch roles after each stretch. Have your partner checkoff below when each stretch has been performed properly. If you have questions or need assistance, contact your instructor.

1. Lower back and hamstring stretch 1
2. Lower back and hamstring stretch 2
3. Quadriceps stretch 1
4. Quadriceps stretch 2
5. Overhead stretch
6. Trunk twist stretch

Partner's initials _____ Date completed _____

MODULE 2

DRIBBLING

POSSESSION OF THE BALL: BASIC DRIBBLING

INTRODUCTION

Possession of the ball is one key to becoming a successful soccer player. Dribbling is considered a major skill in soccer and the prime skill for possessing the ball. Dribbling is an effective method of moving the ball around the field and, by controlling the ball, allows you and your teammates the opportunity to score goals. The ability to maneuver the ball while maintaining control happens continuously throughout the game. Dribbling is best learned in a dynamic setting involving other players. Focusing on your ability to control the ball among other players in a confined space will enable you to dribble confidently in a game situation. Dribbling is not done in a straight line. Effective dribblers must be able to change speeds and directions while maintaining control. Groups of six players (each with his or her own ball) should concentrate on dribbling the ball in a 20 by 20 yards space.

INSTRUCTOR DEMONSTRATION

Your course instructor will demonstrate each recommended technique for dribbling. If you have questions, be sure to ask them before proceeding to the individualized task sequence. Refer to Photos 2.2A through D as your instructor explains and demonstrates each performance cue for dribbling.

Photos 2.2A through D
Top of foot dribble, with stop

A

B

C

D

PERFORMANCE CUES

1. Keep the ball close while moving in a confined space.
2. Keep your head up as much as possible to be aware of other dribblers (in game play it will be opponents) and open spaces.
3. Be able to place your foot on top of the ball immediately following the stop or freeze command.
4. Use all parts of both feet to control the ball.
5. Change speed and directions often.

READINESS DRILLS

2-1. Get into a group of six players, each with his or her own ball. Follow the performance cues and execute them within your group by drib-

Photo 2.3
Readiness Drill 2-1

bling in a space that is either 20 by 20 yards square or in a circle that has a diameter of 20 yards. See Photo 2.3 Each group should complete six 40-second bouts of dribbling. Demonstrate effective dribbling by maintaining the ball within the designated space, changing speeds and directions, using all parts of the foot, and avoiding running into other dribblers.

2-2.   In a group of six with one member acting as an observer, complete six 40-second bouts of dribbling that include two "Stop" signals called out by the observer in each bout. Each member of the group observes one 40-second bout. Control of the ball (putting a foot on top of the ball within 2 seconds of the command) should be demonstrated by each group member. As soon as all group members have placed a foot on the ball, a "Go" call can be given for all group members to resume dribbling.

If you experience difficulty with the readiness drills, refer to the **Performance Cues** and review each one as presented. If you still have difficulty, ask your course instructor to assist you in applying these techniques.

Common Errors and Their Correction

Error	Correction
Attempting to dribble too fast, leading to a lack of control.	Slow down to a speed at which you can maintain control.
Dribbling with head down, making it difficult to spot opponents or an open space.	Try to keep head up in order to see where opponents (other dribblers) are, as well as to identify open space in which to take the ball.
Dribbling in a straight line or in a circle.	This does not happen when playing soccer, so it is important to play in a 360-degree environment (moving in all directions).

CRITERION TASK 2-1

Partner-Checked

In a group of six, with each member acting as an observer for one trial period, perform six successful 40-second dribbling trials using all parts of the feet, all available space, changing speed and direction, and stopping on command at least 2 times. Control will be demonstrated by being able to stop the ball within 2 seconds after the observer gives the "Stop" command. The space for this activity should be a 20 by 20 yard square or a circle with a diameter of 20 yards. Mark this area with cones or other markers. Have the observer monitor the success of each player and write his or her initials after each success trial. This criterion task is complete when you have recorded six successful trials.

Successful trials	1	2	3	4	5	6
Observer's initials						

Date completed _____

SPEED DRIBBLING

INTRODUCTION

The ability to dribble at speed is very important, especially if passing or shooting is not an option. The ability of a player to quickly maneuver the ball through an area of the field can be most useful to a team. A defender can dribble the ball out of danger, and an attacking player can take the ball quickly and under control toward the goal.

INSTRUCTOR DEMONSTRATION

Your course instructor will demonstrate each recommended technique for speed dribbling. If you have questions, be sure to ask them before proceeding to the individualized task sequence. Refer to Photo 2.4 as your instructor explains and demonstrates each performance cue for speed dribbling.

Photo 2.4
Speed dribbling

PERFORMANCE CUES

1. Use the top of the foot to control the pace of the ball.
2. Use light touches to keep the ball near the feet (within 5 feet when moving forward).
3. Move in a forward direction at a speed that will allow you to maintain control.

READINESS DRILL

2-3. Alternating with a partner, dribble the ball a distance of 20 yards to a marker (cone) and return using the top of the foot. Try to increase your pace while maintaining control of the ball. Set a goal of 25 seconds or less to dribble to the marker and back. Attempt nine trials, three utilizing the top of your right foot, three utilizing the top of your left foot, and three alternating the tops of both feet during the trial.

Common Errors and Their Correction

Error	Correction
Attempting to dribble too fast, leading to a lack of control.	Slow down to a speed at which you can maintain control.
Striking the ball too hard, causing a loss of control.	Touch the ball gently with the top of the foot so that it stays close to you.
Dribbling in a straight line or in a circle.	This does not happen when playing soccer, so it is important to play in a 360-degree environment (moving in all directions).

If you experience difficulty with the readiness drill, refer to the **Performance Cues** and review each one as presented. If you still have difficulty, ask your course instructor to assist you in applying these techniques.

CRITERION TASK 2-2

Partner-Checked

Alternating with a partner, dribble a distance of 20 yards to a marker (cone) and return using the tops of either foot. To complete this task, you must accumulate a total of three trials completed in less than 25 seconds. To demonstrate control, the ball must be stopped within 2 feet of the marker at the start or finish line. Have your partner initial each successful trial. This criterion task is complete when you have recorded six successful trials.

Successful trials	1	2	3	4	5	6
Observer's initials						

Date completed _____

SPACE AWARENESS WHILE DRIBBLING

INTRODUCTION

Dribbling is a dynamic activity that involves maneuvering the ball while keeping control and changing speeds and directions. It is essential for soccer players to be aware of their environment when dribbling in order to determine when it is beneficial to protect the ball from an opponent, dribble into open space, pass to an open teammate, or take a shot at the goal. A player in possession of the ball must be able to keep her or his head up in order to take advantage of opportunities that arise during play.

INSTRUCTOR DEMONSTRATION

Your course instructor will demonstrate each recommended technique for developing space awareness and shielding while dribbling. If you have questions, be sure to ask them before proceeding to the individualized task sequence. Refer to Photos 2.5A and B as your instructor explains and demonstrates each performance cue for shielding while you dribble.

Photo 2.5A
Shielding, foot on ball

Photo 2.5B
Shielding, foot next to ball

PERFORMANCE CUES

1. Shield the ball (protect it) when confronted by an opponent by keeping your body between the ball and your opponent.
2. You will need to move your body and your feet as you change direction.
3. Keep the ball close (within 3 feet) while protecting it.

READINESS DRILL

2-4.   In a group of three players, one will possess the ball, one will act as a defender, and one will act as an observer and timer. The object of the drill is to possess the ball in a 20 by 20 yard square or circle with a 20 - yard diameter. You may choose to start with a slightly smaller space initially. Keep the ball from your partner (shielding) for a period of 20 seconds. Perform 10 trials each, changing roles (offense, defense, or observer) after each trial. The observer will signal when to start and stop and offer suggestions (performance cues) to each player. If the ability to possess the ball for 20 seconds is established for five consecutive trials, increase the trial time to 30 seconds.

If you experience difficulty with the readiness drill, refer to the **Performance Cues** and review each one as presented. If you still have difficulty, ask your course instructor to assist you in applying these techniques.

Common Errors and Their Correction

Error	Correction
Watching the ball may cause a loss of awareness of your opponent.	1. Try to keep head up, identifying where your opponent is and what your opportunities may be (passing or shooting).
	2. Glance at the ball periodically while keeping your body between the ball and your opponent.
The ball strays too far away from you.	Keep the ball close enough to reach out and touch.

CRITERION TASK 2-3

Partner-Checked

In a group of three players and in a 20 by 20 yard square or a circle with a 20-yard diameter, each player is to perform three successful trials demonstrating proper shielding technique for a period of 20 seconds. One player will be in possession of the ball, one will act as the defender, and one will observe and keep the time. Players will switch positions after each trial. Have the observer initial each successful trial. This criterion task is complete when you have recorded six successful trials.

Successful trials	1	2	3	4	5	6
Observer's initials						

Date completed _____

MODULE 3

TACKLING

INTRODUCTION

Tackling in soccer means taking the ball directly away from an opponent. The methods of tackling are as varied as those of dribbling, but there are some generally accepted methods that are explained in more detail here. The ability to dispossess the ball from an opponent is an important skill that all players must master. Tackling is more than just kicking the ball away. It is a method to win possession. We will focus on the basic tackle that should always be utilized when the player with the ball is coming directly toward the defender.

When a player with the ball approaches, the defender must take a position directly in front to block the intended path. The tackle is made with the inside part of the foot. The weight is placed on the standing foot, which is slightly bent at the knee and pointed forward. The tackling foot must be turned outward at a 90-degree angle and is bent at the knee, raising the foot slightly off the ground (3 to 5 inches). At the moment the foot makes contact with the ball (which is at the feet of the dribbler), the upper body is inclined slightly forward and the head is looking down at the ball. The arms are away from the body and used for balance.

The tackling foot is swung backward slightly and, with the muscles and joints tightened, the tackling foot is placed directly in the path of the ball as if to strike it with the inside part of the foot. On contact, the tackling foot is used to push the ball in the opposite direction.

INSTRUCTOR DEMONSTRATION

Your course instructor will demonstrate each recommended technique for tackling. If you have questions, be sure to ask them before proceeding to the individualized task sequence. Note each of the performance cues below as your instructor explains and demonstrates the basic tackling skill.

PERFORMANCE CUES

1. The basic tackle is made head-on with the attacking player.
2. The support foot is pointed forward and is slightly bent.
3. The tackling foot is turned at a 90-degree angle and the knee is slightly bent, lifting the foot off the ground 3 to 5 inches.
4. The upper body is bent slightly forward and the head is pointed down.
5. Muscles and joints are made stiff on contact, and the ball is struck in the center with the inside part of the foot.
6. Attempt to play the ball back in the direction it came from.

READINESS DRILLS

3-1. In groups of three, two players stand facing each other with a ball placed between them. The third player is an observer and signals when to start. The practicing players stand a little to the side of the ball so that the standing foot of each player is roughly in line with the ball. On a signal from the observer, both players move their tackling foot forward and attempt to simultaneously strike the ball with the inside of the foot. On contact, each player tries to win possession of the ball. Each player should attempt five trials before rotating players. Each player should complete 10 trials.

3-2. In a pair, player A (with the ball) attacks player B (the tackler), first at a walking pace from 10 yards and then at a jog trot from the same distance. Player B places the inside of his or her tackling foot into the path of the ball and attempts to win possession. Each player should attempt five trials before rotating positions. Each player should complete 10 trials of both the walking pace and jog-trot pace. Be very careful not to attack too aggressively and possibly hurt the player with the ball. This is only a drill!

Common Errors and Their Correction

Error	Correction
Placing weight on tackling foot.	Tackle the ball while keeping weight on the standing foot.
Leaning backward or standing upright when tackling, placing the tackler in an awkward position with less chance of success.	Lean forward when initiating tackle.
Tensing or tightening the muscles of the tackling foot and leg. This may lead to injury.	Attempt to stay relaxed, as if sliding under control.

MODULE 4

FEINTING

INTRODUCTION

Feinting, or faking, is an action designed to elude or deceive an opponent. This action can be done with and without the ball. It often happens in a game when a player is under pressure or is attempting to move into a space to receive the ball. In these situations it is necessary to attempt to *unweight* (cause to become off balance) an opponent thereby creating time and space in which to play. This module will involve two components: (1) feinting without the ball, and (2) feinting with the ball.

FEINTING WITHOUT THE BALL

Feinting may be defined as the art of making movements designed to mask the real intended movement. The essential component is to get an opponent to make a false move, that is, get the opponent to move one way while you move another. If the feint is genuine, the opponent will "bite" and you will have created your opportunity to relieve the defensive pressure and move into a space to receive a pass.

FEINTING WITH THE BALL

The same feinting techniques used without the ball are used while in possession of it. The key is to maintain possession while feinting. It is important to "sell" the feint to an opponent and then quickly move with the ball into space you have created for yourself.

INSTRUCTOR DEMONSTRATION

Your course instructor will demonstrate each recommended technique for feinting, with and without the ball. If you have questions, be sure to ask them before proceeding to the individualized task sequence. Refer to Photos 4.1A through C (shown with ball) as your instructor explains and demonstrates each performance cue for feinting.

Photos 4.1A through C
Feinting with ball

A

B

C

PERFORMANCE CUES

1. When not in possession of the ball, quickly move one way and then another to try to gain a space advantage.
2. When possessing the ball, quickly move one way and then another and try to gain a space advantage while maintaining control of the ball.

READINESS DRILLS

4-1.   Form a group of three. With one partner, play a game of "back tag" in a 20 by 20 yard square or in a circle with a 20-yard diameter *without using a ball*. The tag game goes on for 30 seconds. Each player is "it" and each attempts to tag her or his partner *in the back*. The third player keeps the time and rotates in after each 30-second game. Feints and fakes are required. There should be a minimum of five 30-second trials for each player.

4-2.   Same as Readiness Drill 4-1, except each player possesses a ball and attempts to tag his or her partner *in the back only* while using feints and fakes to avoid being tagged or to create an opportunity to successfully tag the partner. The third member of the group keeps time and rotates in after each 30-second trial. There should be a minimum of five 30-second trials for each player.

4-3.   In a group of six players in a 20 by 20 yard square or a circle with a 20-yard diameter, play a game of "everybody is it" *without using a ball*. Players will use feints and fakes and attempt to tag everyone in the group as many times as possible and at the same time avoid being tagged. *Tags may be on the shoulders or back only.* The period of the game should be for 1 minute, and a minimum of five trials should be conducted by each player.

4-4.   Same as Readiness Drill 4-3, but everyone possesses a ball and attempts to retain possession of it while using feints and fakes to avoid being tagged. Players also attempt to tag other members of the group *in the back and shoulder area only*. The period of the game should be for 1 minute and a minimum of five trials should be conducted by each player.

If you experience difficulty with the readiness tasks, please refer to the **Performance Cues** and review each cue as presented. If you still have difficulty, ask your instructor to assist you in applying these techniques.

Common Errors and Their Correction

Error	Correction
Slow movements may not *unweight* an opponent.	Move quickly when performing a feint.
Failure to "sell" the feint may not get the opponent to "bite".	Overemphasize the feint.
Losing control or possession of the ball.	Concentrate on feinting and controlling the ball first without pressure from an opponent (practice moving one way and then taking the ball another way without a defender present). Once comfortable, add the pressure of a defender.

MODULE **5**

KICKING AND RECEIVING

INTRODUCTION

One player kicks the soccer ball to another player, who receives it. These are the opposite ends of the same skill sequence, which will be learned in this module. Kicking and receiving go together like passing and catching in many other sports; they are how one player projects the ball to another player, who then gains control of the ball to either dribble it, shoot it, or pass it to another teammate.

KICKING

Kicking is the conscious striking of the ball with some part of the foot. It is a fundamental technical element used to play the ball to a teammate, play the ball out of a dangerous area, or shoot the ball at the goal. Accuracy is most important. The basic kick technique utilizes a three-step approach beginning with your nonkicking (nondominant) foot. Your first two steps are toward the ball, and your third step (nonkicking foot) is placed next to the ball (3 to 6 inches away) and will be pointed at your intended target (partner). Your eyes are on the ball.

When placing your nonkicking foot next to the ball, swing your kicking foot in a motion to strike the ball in the center with the inside part of the foot. Your kicking foot should have the toe pointed approximately 90 degrees away from your target, exposing the largest part of your foot (inside) to the ball. The ankle of your kicking foot should be firm (locked) as you strike the ball. The leg will also be turned outwards from the hip so that the horizontal plane of the foot runs parallel to the ground. The knee of the kicking foot is slightly bent so that the foot is 3 to 5 inches off the ground.

Your upper body is bent slightly forward, providing momentum toward your target. Your arms are at your sides, slightly away from the body, to provide balance. They move very little throughout the kicking motion. After you strike the ball, your kicking foot continues in the direction of your target in a follow-through motion.

INSTRUCTOR DEMONSTRATION

Your course instructor will demonstrate each recommended technique for kicking. If you have questions, be sure to ask them before proceeding to the individualized task sequence. Refer to Photos 5.1A and B as your instructor explains and demonstrates each performance cue for kicking.

Photo 5.1A
Kick, contact

Photo 5.1B
Kick, follow-through

PERFORMANCE CUES FOR KICKING

1. Keep your eyes on the ball.
2. Place nonkicking foot next to the ball and point it at your target.
3. Lock your kicking ankle and turn 90 degrees from your target.
4. Strike the ball in the center.
5. Your upper body moves forward towards the target after contact.

RECEIVING THE BALL

Receiving the ball can be defined as the skill of trapping or stopping a moving ball for the purpose of controlling it. Receiving the ball is one of the most important techniques of the game, and it involves numerous body parts. This skill sequence will focus on receiving the ball with the inside part of the foot.

When executing an inside of the foot trap, stand facing your partner who is passing the ball to you. Be ready to receive it with either foot. As the ball is played, move toward it by taking one or two small steps. Prepare the leg and foot you wish to receive the ball with by turning the leg outward at the hip, bending the knee slightly which will bring the foot 3 to 5 inches off the ground, and pointing the toe approximately 90 degrees away from the path of the ball.

The foot should be offered to the ball and the upper body should be bent slightly forward. The foot and ankle should be firm (locked) as the ball arrives. As the ball contacts the receiving foot, the foot should be pulled back slightly and relaxed to help absorb the force of the ball. This will help in controlling the pass and keep the ball from bouncing away.

INSTRUCTOR DEMONSTRATION

Your course instructor will demonstrate each recommended technique for receiving. If you have questions, be sure to ask them before proceeding to the individualized task sequence. Refer to Photos 5.2A through C as your instructor explains and demonstrates each performance cue for receiving.

Photo 5.2A
Inside foot reception, preparation (receiver on right)

Photo 5.2B
Inside foot reception, contact

Photo 5.2C
Inside foot reception, foot on top for control

PERFORMANCE CUES FOR RECEIVING

1. Move forward to meet the ball and keep eyes focused on it.
2. Prepare to receive the ball by moving forward to meet it.
3. Prepare to receive the ball with either foot.
4. Receiving foot is made stiff (locked) and turned at a right angle (90 degrees).
5. Upon contact, relax the foot and "give" to deaden the ball.
6. Place foot on top of ball for control.

READINESS DRILLS

5-1.   With a partner, stand approximately 10 paces (25 to 30 feet) apart and utilize one ball between you. Use a cone to mark this distance. You and your partner will combine an inside of the foot kick (pass) with an inside of the foot reception (trap). Each player should complete two trials of 25 successful kicks and receptions with each foot. Partners should place their own initials in the space below after each trial.

   _____   _____
   Trial 1 Right Foot   Trial 1 Left Foot

   _____   _____
   Trial 2 Right Foot   Trial 2 Left Foot

   Date completed _____

5-2.   In a group of six players, divide into two groups of three and play a possession game (keep away) in a space that is 30 by 30 yards square. Play until both groups have successfully completed six pass and receive combinations within their group. Each successful pass and reception counts as one of the six needed. Interchange players between groups if desired.

   _____   _____
   Group members' initials   Date completed

If you experience difficulty with the readiness drill, refer to the **Performance Cues** and review each cue as presented. If you still have difficulty, ask your course instructor to assist you in applying these techniques.

Common Errors and Their Correction: Kicking

Error	Correction
Ball off target line.	Be sure your support foot is next to the ball and pointed at your target when kicking.
Bouncing ball, caused by striking the ball above its center.	Strike the ball at center by watching foot make contact.
Ball kicked in the air, caused by leaning back on contact and getting "too fat" under it.	1. Lean forward at contact. 2. Strike the ball at center by watching foot make contact.
Lack of power.	Follow through towards your target after the kick to assure maximum power.

Common Errors and Their Correction: Receiving

Error	Correction
Ball bounces away after initial contact.	Relax and "give" on contact. The foot and leg are often too stiff and the ball rebounds on contact.
Ball hits the toe or shin.	1. Turn receiving foot to 90 degrees away from path of the ball. 2. Move forward to meet the ball.

CHALLENGE GAMES FOR DRIBBLING, PASSING, AND RECEIVING

INTRODUCTION

Dribbling, passing, and receiving happen constantly throughout a soccer game. The following sequence of exercises, performed with a group of team-mates, will help you link the individual skills and utilize them in a soccer game. One of the best ways to link these skills is to play small-sided games. Follow the sequence of these complex exercises in the Challenge Games as explained.

When participating in challenge tasks, it is important to perform them in a manner as close to the actual game as possible. In a game of soccer, drib-bling, passing, receiving, tackling, shooting, heading, and the skills of a goal-keeper are interrelated and happen continuously during play. It is important for a player to be able to combine all the individual skill components in a gamelike environment.

The instructional setting for the following challenge games is a small-sided game with specific objectives. Each game features one group of six play-ers in a space that is 30 yards square. The group of six will perform skills in an active mode inside the space. It is important for each member of the group to assist his or her teammates to learn these tasks. In these exercises, tactics and strategies are introduced. The basic tactical premise in soccer is simple: when in possession of the ball, we work as a team to attack the opponent's goal, and when we are not in possession of the ball, we work as a team to defend our goal and win the ball back.

INSTRUCTOR DEMONSTRATION

Your course instructor will review each recommended dribbling, feinting, passing, and receiving skill you have learned so far as they are applied in a gamelike situation. Observe the demonstrations carefully, making note of the game structures that follow.

CHALLENGE GAME 5-1

Six players, all on the same team, are in a 30 by 30 yard square space. Mark off the space with cones at each corner (see Photo 5.3). Each player is assigned a number, 1 through 6. Player 1 has the ball and begins dribbling. The remaining five players move slowly within the space. Player 2 signals (verbally and by moving toward player 1) when he or she is ready to receive a pass. When eye contact is made, player 1 passes the ball to player 2 who must receive it correctly by utilizing an inside of the foot reception (trap). Player 2 begins to dribble and follows the same procedure with player 3, and so on through player 6. Player 6 plays the ball to player 1 and the sequence begins again. Each player should dribble the ball for about 10 seconds before passing it while the other players move in the designated space. The sequence should be completed 3 times. It is important for the players to utilize the entire space available for this exercise. Recommended distance for passing to a teammate is 10 yards. To engage more players in dribbling, passing, and receiving, a second ball can be added to the sequence.

Photo 5.3
Challenge Game 5-1

CHALLENGE GAME 5-2

Use the same space and six-player team as for Challenge Game 5-1. Each player is assigned a number 1 through 6. Player 1 has the ball and begins to dribble. He or she must identify player 2 and, on eye contact, deliver an inside of the foot pass to player 2. Instead of controlling the ball as before, player 2 plays a one-touch pass back to player #1, who receives the ball, controls it, begins to dribble, and makes contact with player 3, with whom the same sequence happens. This continues until all five players have received a pass and played a one-touch pass back to player 1. The sequence continues with player 2 following the same procedure. Recommended distance for passing to a teammate is 10 yards. To engage more players in dribbling, passing, and receiving, a second ball can be added to the sequence.

CHALLENGE GAME 5-3

Six players, *split into two groups of three*, play in the same 30 by 30 yard space used for the previous games. This three versus three game stresses dribbling, passing, and receiving, and the use of feints and fakes is encouraged. There are four goals, one at the midpoint between each corner cone. You can use a mini-goal like the one shown in Photo 5.4 or you can place cones about 9 feet apart to serve as goals. Each team of three must defend two goals and attack two goals, so the game can go in many directions. The goals to defend and attack are agreed on before the game begins. The ball must stay on or near the ground and be no more than knee-high for the goal to count. Each game is 6 minutes in length, and a total of three games should be played.

Photo 5.4
Challenge Game 5-3

MODULE 6

THE INSTEP DRIVE

INTRODUCTION

The instep drive involves a kick of the ball using the area of the foot between the base of the toes and the curve of the ankle. Simply, it is the area of the foot covered by the shoelaces and is commonly referred to as the instep. This kick is used to generate power and if needed, distance. It is the preferred method of shooting for a goal and is also commonly used to make long-distance passes. Defenders can use the instep drive to clear the ball out of dangerous areas. Goal kicks and corner kicks are most often made using an instep drive.

Place the ball 6 to 7 yards in front of you and keep your eyes focused on the ball during the kicking process. Approach the ball from a slight angle to the side of your nonkicking foot. Utilize a small step approach until the last step, which will be taken with the non-kicking foot and will be a long stride. Your last step is placed next to the ball (3 to 6 inches away) and pointed at your target (goal).

Upon placing your nonkicking foot next to the ball, swing your kicking foot in a motion to strike the ball in its center with the instep part of your foot. The toes of the kicking foot should be pointed approximately 45 degrees down and away from the contact area (center) of the ball. Your ankle should be firm or stiff (locked) as you strike the ball. The leg is swung forward powerfully from the hip. The foot stays angled down and locked until the kick is completed. The knee of the kicking foot is slightly bent on contact and straightens during the follow-through.

Your upper body is bent slightly forward, providing momentum toward your target. Your arms provide balance, and there is some movement forward of the arm opposite the kicking foot during the kicking motion. If the ball is to be kept low, the knee of the kicking foot is bent and over the ball. If a medium high ball is desired, the support foot is placed slightly behind the ball, and the ball is contacted slightly below the center.

INSTRUCTOR DEMONSTRATION

Your course instructor will demonstrate each recommended technique for the instep drive. If you have questions, be sure to ask them before proceeding to the individualized task sequence. Refer to Photos 6.1A through D as your instructor explains and demonstrates each performance cue for this skill.

Photo 6.1A
Instep drive, approach

Photo 6.1B
Instep drive, precontact

Photo 6.1C
Instep drive, contact

Photo 6.1D
Instep drive, follow-through

PERFORMANCE CUES

1. Your last step is a long stride with your nonkicking leg.
2. Place your nonkicking foot next to the ball.
3. Lock the ankle of your kicking foot and hold it down and away at a 45-degree angle.
4. The kicking foot knee is bent slightly on contact and straightens on follow-through.
5. The upper body is bent forward at the waist and momentum is directed toward the target.
6. The arms are held away from the body for balance.

READINESS DRILL

6-1. Get in a group of six players. Two players, with three balls each, place the ball approximately 10 yards in front of a regulation goal (with nets), and kick shots to the goal).* The other players assist in retrieving and returning balls to the shooter. After nine instep drives into the goal, players change positions. Each player should attempt 36 instep drives with her or his dominant foot. Players count the number of successful instep drives, with an eventual goal of 7 out of 9 balls struck firmly and accurately.

*If a regulation goal with nets is not available, practice by striking the ball with the instep to a partner who is 25 to 30 yards away. Strike the ball hard and with accuracy. Partners should adjust their positions accordingly. Each player should strike 36 balls with the instep of her or his dominant foot. Partners practice their receiving skills once the ball is struck toward them.

READINESS DRILL

6-2. With a setup similar to Readiness Drill 6-1, each player practices striking the ball with the instep of the nondominant foot. This is more difficult for most players, and success can be measured with an objective of 5 out of 9 balls struck firmly and accurately.

If you experience difficulty with the readiness drills, refer to the **Performance Cues** and review each cue as presented. If you still have difficulty, ask your course instructor to assist you in applying these techniques.

Common Errors and Their Correction

Error	Correction
Ball kicked off the intended line.	1. The angle of approach may be too sharp; decrease the angle of approach. 2. The support foot may not be pointed to the intended target; be sure the foot is placed next to or slightly behind the ball and is pointed at the intended target.
Loss of power and accuracy.	1. The kicking ankle may not be held firmly enough during contact with the ball; lock the ankle throughout the kicking motion. 2. The ball may be struck off center; strike the ball in the center to keep the ball close to the ground.
Ball flies higher than intended.	1. Caused by leaning back too far at contact, and ball is stuck below center. Lean forward going into contact with ball.

CRITERION TASK 6-1

Partner-Checked

Practice this task with a partner so that you can help each other retrieve balls for more practice attempts. Place a cone or other marker 10 yards from the front of the goal. If a goal is not available, you can use two cones placed against a wall, set to the distance between two regulation goalposts. Practice taking instep drives at the goal with your dominant foot in blocks of 10 shots. *A shot is not successful if it bounces before crossing into the goal.* Record the number of successful shots for each block on the **Personal Recording Form**. When four individual block scores reach or exceed 7 out of 10, have your partner initial and date in the space provided.

Personal Recording Form									
Block 1	Block 2	Block 3	Block 4	Block 5	Block 6	Block 7	Block 8	Block 9	Block 10
___/10	___/10	___/10	___/10	___/10	___/10	___/10	___/10	___/10	___/10

Your partner's initials _____   Date completed _____

CRITERION TASK 6-2

Partner-Checked

Practice this task with a partner so that you can help each other retrieve balls for more practice attempts. Place a cone or other marker 10 yards from the front of the goal. If a goal is not available, you can use two cones placed against a wall, set to the distance between two regulation goalposts. Practice taking instep drives at the goal with your nondominant foot in blocks of 10 shots. *A shot is not successful if it bounces before crossing into the goal.* Record the number of successful shots for each block on the **Personal Recording Form**. When four individual block scores reach or exceed 5 out of 10, have your partner initial and date in the space provided.

Personal Recording Form									
Block 1	Block 2	Block 3	Block 4	Block 5	Block 6	Block 7	Block 8	Block 9	Block 10
___/10	___/10	___/10	___/10	___/10	___/10	___/10	___/10	___/10	___/10

Your partner's initials _____   Date completed _____

MODULE 7

RECEIVING THE BALL
WITH THE UPPER BODY

INTRODUCTION

In soccer, the ball is played on the ground and in the air. When played on the ground it is effectively received with the feet, as you have already learned. When played in the air or if it is bouncing, it is necessary to play the ball with some other part of the body (contact with hands and arms is illegal!). Nearly any part of the body above the feet can be utilized to receive the ball for the purpose of possession. The two most common areas used to receive the ball are the thigh and the chest.

THIGH TRAP

The thigh area (quadriceps muscle) is a thick muscle that presents a big surface to contact the ball and also helps take the pace out of the ball, making it easier to control. The player receiving the ball with the thigh faces in the direction from which the ball is coming and positions the body so that the ball will be contacted about waist-high. This takes some adjustment to the pace and flight characteristics of the ball (try to determine where it will come down). Once the body is in position to contact the ball with the thigh, the player must adjust his or her position by placing most of the weight on the support leg and bending the receiving leg at the knee and hip so that the thigh is presented to the ball. This angle is about 60 degrees but can be changed based on the height of the incoming ball.

In this position, the thigh presents a large target for the ball. As the ball contacts the thigh, the player must relax the leg to help absorb the force of the ball. On contact, the player should "give" or pull the leg back. This technique also helps deaden the ball and the motion allows the ball to drop to the feet quickly but softly.

INSTRUCTOR DEMONSTRATION

Your course instructor will demonstrate each recommended technique for the thigh trap. If you have questions, be sure to ask them before proceeding to the individualized task sequence. Refer to Photos 7.1A and B as your instructor explains and demonstrates each performance cue for this skill.

Photo 7.1A
Thigh trap, positioning

Photo 7.1B
Thigh trap, contact

PERFORMANCE CUES

1. Position the body in the direction of the incoming ball and adjust to receive the ball on the thigh.
2. Keep your eyes on the ball as it approaches; do not look at the defenders.
3. Place your weight on the support leg and provide a wide, balanced stance.
4. Use your arms for additional balance.
5. On contact, relax the thigh and "give" with the ball.
6. Immediately take the thigh away and allow the ball to drop quickly and softly at your feet.

READINESS DRILL

7-1. With a partner and one ball, stand 4 to 6 yards apart. One player tosses the ball in an arc that will arrive at his or her partner's waist. The receiving player must adjust his or her position to effectively trap the ball with the thigh. A trap is successful if the ball is deadened, drops to the ground in front the player, and is in a position where a foot can be placed on the ball before it moves more than 1 yard away from the player. Each player performs 10 successful thigh traps with each thigh.

Common Errors and Their Correction

Error	Correction
Ball did not strike the thigh.	1. Review positioning and practice without the ball. 2. Be sure to relax the thigh on contact.
Ball bounces up in the air.	1. Take the thigh *away*, not toward the ball, on contact.

CHEST TRAP

The other common method for receiving a ball in flight is the chest trap. A chest trap is utilized when the arriving ball is too high for the feet or legs, the ball needs to be possessed, and heading it might prove too risky (the ball may be too low to head safely or possession might be difficult to maintain if the ball is headed). The chest provides a large contact area and is a softer surface than the head or lower leg.

The player receiving the ball must position his or her body in the path of the ball and prepare to receive it with the chest. The ball may be falling from a height above the head or be coming at the chest in a straight line. The player must also judge the pace of the ball. If it is coming at you hard and fast, it may be very difficult to trap the ball with the chest. To trap the ball with the chest, the player needs to adopt a wide stance (wider than shoulder-width) and bend both knees slightly. The weight is evenly distributed on both legs. The hips are thrust slightly forward and the upper body is bent slightly backward at the waist. The chest is relaxed and in a position to contact the ball. The arms are raised for balance and the eyes are on the ball.

The ball should strike the upper chest area near the sternum. As the ball makes contact, there is a straightening of the legs and a forward push of the hips. The upper body moves forward after the initial force of the ball has been absorbed. As with a thigh trap, the player has to relax and "give" with the ball upon contact. The ball should deaden itself against the chest or pop up slightly (a few inches). As the chest comes forward, the ball should fall straight down toward the ground quickly but softly to a position directly in front of the feet.

INSTRUCTOR DEMONSTRATION

Your course instructor will demonstrate each recommended technique for the chest trap. If you have questions, be sure to ask them before proceeding to the individualized task sequence. Refer to Photos 7.2A and B as your instructor explains and demonstrates each performance cue for this skill.

Photo 7.2A
Chest trap, positioning

Photo 7.2B
Chest trap, contact

PERFORMANCE CUES

1. Position the body to receive the ball on the chest; keep your eyes on the ball.
2. Use a wide balanced stance with the weight evenly distributed on both legs.
3. Bend your knees and bring your hips forward. Bend you upper body backward at the waist.
4. Relax and "give" with the ball on contact.
5. Bring your chest forward and allow the ball to drop to your feet.

READINESS TASK

7-2.   With a partner and one ball, stand 4 to 6 yards apart. One player tosses lofted balls that are approximately upper chest in height to his or her partner. The receiving player will have to adjust his or her position to effectively trap the ball with the chest. A trap is successful if the ball is deadened, falls to the ground in front of the player, and is in a position where the player can place a foot on top of the ball before it moves more than 1 yard away. Each player performs 15 successful chest traps.

Common Errors and Their Correction

Error	Correction
Ball bounces off chest.	Be sure to arch your back and relax on contact.
Ball strikes an area of the body other than your chest.	1. Keep your eyes on the ball. 2. Adjust the position of feet and body based on the flight and pace of the ball.
Unable to control the ball after it strikes the chest.	"Give" with the ball and bring the chest slightly forward to allow it to drop to the feet.

CRITERION TASK 7-1

Partner-Checked

Find a practice partner for this task. Set up two cones or other markers about 6 to 8 yards apart. Your partner will make tosses to you, with some being higher and some being lower, in random order. Use the correct trap (thigh or chest) for each ball when it comes to you. A trap is scored as successful if you use the correct trapping technique and can control the ball with one foot before it goes more than one step away from you. Practice this task in blocks of 10 tosses, and record the number of successful traps for each block on the **Personal Recording Form**. When three individual block scores reach or exceed 7 out of 10, have your partner initial and date in the space provided.

Personal Recording Form									
Block 1	Block 2	Block 3	Block 4	Block 5	Block 6	Block 7	Block 8	Block 9	Block 10
___/10	___/10	___/10	___/10	___/10	___/10	___/10	___/10	___/10	___/10

Your partner's initials _____ Date completed _____

CHALLENGE GAME FOR RECEIVING, DRIBBLING, AND SHOOTING

INSTRUCTOR DEMONSTRATION

Your course instructor will review each receiving, dribbling, and shooting, skill you have learned so far, as they are applied in a gamelike situation. Observe the demonstrations carefully, making note of the game structure that follows.

CHALLENGE GAME 7-1

Six to eight players will occupy a 30 by 30-yard space with full-sized goals located on two ends. Another player or the instructor will act as a server and will stand at the side of the field with a minimum of six soccer balls ready for use. The six to eight players will be split into two groups of three or four with one group wearing same-color scrimmage vests (See Photo 7.3). The game begins with the server tossing a ball to one of the players in the game so that it must be controlled with the feet, thigh or chest. *Opponents may not challenge the player receiving the ball until it has been possessed (controlled) or clearly lost.* At this point, the ball is in play, and attempts should be made to evade opponents and create opportunities to score on goals. The player in possession of the ball may also pass to a teammate if it is determined that this will increase the opportunity to score. Once the ball is kicked out of the playing space or if a goal is scored, another ball is tossed in and the sequence begins again. **No goalkeepers are allowed for either team.** The game continues until all balls have been played. If more than two teams of players are ready for this challenge game, they may take turns with the other team after the six balls have been used.

Photo 7.3
Three versus three or four versus four; no goalkeepers

MODULE 8

HEADING

INTRODUCTION

Soccer is unique in that the head is used as both an offensive and defensive weapon. The head is used to control balls that are played in the air. This control leads to possession of the ball, opportunities to score goals, and playing the ball out of danger. There are a wide variety of methods for using the head effectively. The objective here is to understand how to head the ball safely and effectively during game play. Usually there is a target, which may be the goal, a teammate, or a space away from a dangerous area.

In principle, any part of the head can be used to play the ball. Beginning players, however, should learn the skill of heading with the forehead. The front part of the skull is the strongest anatomically and is a relatively even or flat surface, and using this area of the head allows you to visually track the ball up to the moment of impact. By heading with this part of your head, players can also be aware of teammates, opponents, and playing spaces around them. Two keys to successful heading are accuracy and the pace of the ball that is headed.

From a stationary position, the player must be on his or her toes, with legs slightly bent at the knees and the upper body moderately inclined forward from the hips. The arms, which are somewhat bent at the elbows and are held slightly forward and loosely. As the ball approaches, the player must track the ball visually and then move to a position where the ball can be contacted with the head. The body should arch backward and then move forward to contact the ball on the forehead. This allows for momentum and generates power to propel the ball toward its target.

INSTRUCTOR DEMONSTRATION

Your course instructor will demonstrate each recommended technique for heading. If you have questions, be sure to ask them before proceeding to the individualized task sequence. A list of performance cues and photos to accompany this demonstration will appear with each of the following Readiness Drills.

READINESS DRILL

8-1. A player and his or her partner utilize one ball. One player sits on the ground with the legs in a V position. The other player stands approximately 5 feet away, facing the sitting player, holding the ball in her or his hands. The player holding the ball tosses it in an underhand motion to the seated player in such a manner that the ball can be headed back to the thrower's chest. The seated player moves her or his upper body backward at the waist and then moves forward as the ball approaches, striking the ball with the forehead. The target is the abdomen or chest area of the thrower. See Photos 8.1A through C. One player should complete 10 successful headers and then switch roles.

PERFORMANCE CUES

1. Bend backwards at the waist with your eyes tracking the ball.
2. Move forward to strike the ball; do not let it bounce off you.
3. Strike the ball with your forehead, right at the hairline.

Photo 8.1A
Heading from sitting position, preparation

Photo 8.1B
Heading from sitting position, contact

Photo 8.1C
Heading from sitting position, follow-through

READINESS DRILL

8-2.   A second progression for heading is done from a kneeling position, which offers a greater range of motion. Two players again work together with one kneeling in an upright position and one standing approximately 10 feet away facing his or her partner. The standing player tosses the ball in an underhand motion in such a way that the ball can be contacted by the kneeling player's forehead and directed back to the thrower's chest. The kneeling player should lean backward from both knees and the waist and come forward to meet the ball. After contact, the body should continue forward in the direction of the target. Neck and shoulder muscles will tense on contact. Arms are held out for balance and can be used to support the player heading the ball as he or she moves the upper body forward. See Photos 8.2A through C. One player should complete 10 successful headers and then switch roles.

Photo 8.2A
Heading from kneeling position, preparation

Photo 8.2B
Heading from kneeling position, contact

Photo 8.2C
Heading from kneeling position, follow-through

PERFORMANCE CUES

1. Move back initially from the knees and waist.
2. Move forward to strike the ball; do not let it bounce off you.
3. Strike the ball with your forehead at the hairline.
4. Continue forward motion and contact in the direction of your target.

READINESS DRILL

8-3. The third progression is heading from a standing position. Two players with one ball stand approximately 12 to 15 feet apart. Use a cone to mark the distance. One will toss the ball in an underhand motion to his or her partner in such a way that the player can head the ball with the forehead. The player heading the ball must adjust his or her position in relationship to the flight of the ball and keep his orher eyes on it. The upper body is bent backward at the waist, the knees are bent slightly and the player is on his or her toes. As the ball arrives, the upper body moves forward to contact the ball on the forehead. Arms are held out for balance. When positioning to head the ball the player may wish to place one foot slightly more forward than the other. See Photos 8.3A through C. One player should complete 10 successful headers and then switch roles.

Photo 8.3A
Heading from standing position, preparation

Photo 8.3B
Heading from standing position, contact

Photo 8.3C
Heading from standing position, follow-through

PERFORMANCE CUES

1. Eyes are on the ball, knees are slightly bent, and the back is bent backward from the waist.
2. The upper body moves forward as the ball arrives.
3. The ball is truck with the forehead at the hairline.
4. The neck and shoulder muscles will tense on contact.
5. The ball should be directed at your target.

Common Errors and Their Correction

Error	Correction
Ball is offline to target.	1. Body should face target. 2. Ball did not strike the forehead squarely; keep eyes on the ball all the way.
Headache.	Ducking before contact can cause the ball to hit the top of the head, not the forehead.
Lack of pace (power).	Move the body **into** the ball to strike it; do not let the ball just bounce off you.
Lack of control.	Being too tense or too relaxed; tense just before contact.

CRITERION TASK 8-1

Partner-Checked

With a partner, stand 8 to 12 feet away facing each other; your partner has a ball. Your partner jogs backward *slowly* and you jog slowly toward him or her, maintaining the 8 to 12 foot space. Your partner tosses the ball so that you must adjust to the flight of the ball while moving forward and jump up to make contact. The target is the upper chest area of the thrower, no more than one step from him or her. This task should be conducted over a space of 35 to 40 yards. It is not likely that you will move in a straight line, so you need to be aware of other students around you. Practice this task in blocks of 10 shots and record the number of successful shots for each block on the **Personal Recording Form**. When three individual block scores reach or exceed 5 out of 10, have your partner initial and date in the space provided.

Personal Recording Form									
Block 1	Block 2	Block 3	Block 4	Block 5	Block 6	Block 7	Block 8	Block 9	Block 10
__/10	__/10	__/10	__/10	__/10	__/10	__/10	__/10	__/10	__/10

Your partner's initials _____ Date completed _____

MODULE 9

THE THROW-IN

INTRODUCTION

Whenever the ball is played over the touchline (sideline), it is put back into play with a throw-in from the point where it went out of bounds. This is the only time a player other than the goalkeeper can legally play the ball with his or her hands. The player making the throw-in must stand facing the field of play with her or his feet on or behind the touchline. The ball is held firmly with both hands and thrown from a point that begins from behind the head. Both feet *must* remain in contact with the ground throughout the entire throwing motion. There are two methods by which the ball can be legally thrown back into play. One is a throw-in from a standing position; the other is a throw-in after an approach run.

THROW-IN FROM THE STANDING POSITION

To make a legal throw-in, the ball is held firmly and comfortably in both hands with the fingers slightly outspread. The palms face the intended direction of the throw and the thumbs are placed as near to each other as possible. The feet are comfortably placed slightly less than shoulder-width distance apart (10 to 14 inches). The ball is raised over the head with both hands until it touches the back of the neck. The upper body is inclined backward from the hips and the knees are bent. As soon as the body reaches this position, a rapid straightening of the arms is combined with a strong forward movement (toward the intended target) of the upper body. Straightening of the legs gives added power to the throw-in. The ball should not leave the hands until the arms are over the head. A follow-through action is required to complete the throw-in.

INSTRUCTOR DEMONSTRATION

Your course instructor will demonstrate each recommended technique for the throw-in from the standing position. If you have questions, be sure to ask them before proceeding to the individualized task sequence. Refer to Photos 9.1A and B as your instructor explains and demonstrates each performance cue for this skill.

Photo 9.1A
Standing throw-in, preparing
to throw

Photo 9.1B
Standing throw-in, follow-through

PERFORMANCE CUES

1. Place both feet on the ground, either on or behind the touchline and slightly less than shoulder-width apart.
2. The throw must come from behind the head.
3. The ball is held and thrown with equal pressure applied from both hands.
4. Follow through fully, directly toward your target.

READINESS DRILL

9-1. Find a partner and get one ball. Stand approximately 10 to 12 steps apart (25 to 30 feet) and mark the distance with a cone or other marker. The player with the ball attempts to throw the ball (utilizing correct technique) to his or her partner's feet. The ball should be trapped by the receiving player, picked up once controlled, and thrown (correctly) back to the partner. Each player should complete 20 successful throw-ins at this distance. If after five successful throw-ins, you feel you need a greater challenge, each of you takes two step backward, thereby increasing the distance for the throw-in. Remember, your target is your partner's feet. If you find it difficult to reach your partner from the initial distance, take a few steps forward so that you are closer together.

If you experience difficulty with the readiness drill, refer to the **Performance Cues** and review each cue as presented. If you still have difficulty, ask your course instructor to assist you in applying these techniques.

Common Errors and Their Correction

Error	Correction
Clockwise or counterclockwise spin on the ball (this is illegal).	Grip and throw the ball with equal pressure from both hands.
One or both feet come off the ground before release (this is illegal).	Do not lean forward too far or jump to throw the ball.
Just dropping the ball close to yourself (this is illegal).	Use a full follow-through on release.

THROW-IN AFTER AN APPROACH RUN

By taking a short approach run and placing one foot ahead of the other, a longer throw-in can be achieved. The technique for holding and throwing the ball is the same as for the standing throw-in, but there is a more dynamic (lunging) action to the throw-in when a short run (10 to 15 feet) is utilized. After the short run, one foot is placed on or just behind the touchline. The ball is thrown from behind the head with equal pressure applied by both hands. As the ball is released, the follow-through begins. The trailing foot is dragged (toe down) to make sure both feet remain in contact with the ground throughout the throwing motion.

INSTRUCTOR DEMONSTRATION

Your course instructor will demonstrate each recommended technique for the throw-in with an approach run. If you have questions, be sure to ask them before proceeding to the individualized task sequence. Refer to Photos 9.2A through C as your instructor explains and demonstrates each performance cue for this skill.

Photo 9.2A
Running throw-in, end of run

Photo 9.2B
Running throw-in, release

Photo 9.2C
Running throw-in, follow-through

PERFORMANCE CUES

1. After the short approach run, step forward with one foot toward the field of play.
2. The ball is held and thrown with equal pressure from both hands, from behind the head.
3. Momentum is toward the target and the back foot is dragged with the toe down throughout the completion of the throw-in.
4. Follow through fully, directly toward your target.

READINESS DRILL

9-2. Find a partner and get one ball. Use two cones set apart at a distance of 20 to 25 yards. Each partner should stand at one of the cones. The partner with the ball takes a short run and throws the ball correctly to the other partner's feet. That partner traps the ball, gains control, picks up the ball, and completes the same procedure in return. Complete 20 successful throw-ins each. If after five successful throw-ins you feel you need a greater challenge, each of you takes two steps backward, thereby increasing the distance for the throw-in. Remember, you target is your partner's feet. If you find it difficult to reach your partner from the initial distance, take a few steps forward so that you are closer together.

If you experience difficulty with the readiness drill, refer to the **Performance Cues** and review each cue as presented. If you still have difficulty, ask your course instructor to assist you in applying these techniques.

Common Errors and Their Correction

Error	**Correction**
Clockwise or counterclockwise spin on the ball (this is illegal).	Grip and throw the ball with equal pressure from both hands.
Stepping over the touchline with the lead foot (this is illegal).	Check your relationship to the line as you approach it, anticipating that you will need extra room after the run.
Back foot comes off the ground (this is illegal).	1. Do not lean forward too far. 2. Drag the toe of the back foot on the ground.

CHALLENGE GAME FOR THROW-INS, HEADING, AND SHOOTING

INSTRUCTOR DEMONSTRATION

Your course instructor will review the skills for throw-ins, heading, and shooting you have learned so far, as they are applied in a gamelike situation. Observe the demonstrations carefully, making note of the game structure that follows.

CHALLENGE GAME 9-1

You will need two partners, several soccer balls, and a full-sized goal. With cones, mark an area 20 by 20 yards in front of the goal. One player assumes the roll of the shooter, one the roll of the header, and one executes throw-ins. The shooter will stand 15 to 20 yards away from and facing the full-sized goal. The player heading the ball will stand 15 to 20 yards away from and facing the player executing the throw-in who will assume a position outside the space at the midline.

Player A (with the ball) executes a proper throw-in by throwing the ball to player B so that it can be headed to the ground in front of player C. Player C adjusts to the ball and runs on to it, striking the ball (with an instep drive) into the goal.

A successful trial is one in which all three players perform correctly, resulting in a goal. Players perform five trials at each position before rotating clockwise to the next position. The group of three must work as a team to execute each component of this complex technical exercise. Continue the challenge game until all members of the team have completed five successful trials each of the three skills (a total of 15 successful trials).

MODULE 10

GOALKEEPING

INTRODUCTION

The goalkeeper's primary responsibility is to prevent the ball from entering his or her team's goal. The goalkeeper is the one player on the field who is permitted to use the hands to perform this task. It is legal to catch, stop, or deflect (parry) the ball with the hands as long as this occurs inside the penalty area.

Even though a goalkeeper is able to use the hands in the performance of protecting the goal, it is necessary to develop all the basic skills required of field players. The goalkeeper is just like any other player and needs to be able to play the ball during the course of the game. Goalkeepers may even score goals for their team, even though this is an extremely rare occurrence. A Goalkeeper is not only the last line of defense, but is also responsible for initiating the attack once possession of the ball has been gained. Goalkeepers have a distinct advantage in that they can see the entire field of play and all the players—teammates and opponents alike.

The basic goalkeeping skills in this module will be divided into two areas: (1) basic defensive skills, such as catching low, medium, and high balls; and (2) skills for initiating the attack, such as rolling, throwing, and overhand throws to a target.

DEFENSIVE SKILLS

The primary responsibility of the goalkeeper is to serve as the last line of defense for his or her team's goal. Therefore, the development of defensive skills is essential and is covered first in this module. This sequence covers the proper techniques needed for each defensive skill in drill situations, and it is important that you apply these techniques correctly. In a match, however, it is essential that you get the job done (that is, prevent a goal against your team) by any means possible within the rules, which can often mean improvising on each skill as the situation demands.

DEFENSIVE SKILL 1: CATCHING LOW BALLS (BALLS ON THE GROUND)

As the ball approaches the goal, the goalkeeper adjusts his or her focus from a broad scope (seeing the whole field and all the players) to narrow concentration on the ball. Anticipation plays an important part as a goalkeeper attempts to prepare for an attempt by the opponents to score a goal. Part of this anticipation is proper positioning,which is an attempt to place the body between the goal and the anticipated path of the ball and to ready the body to make the save.

The goalkeeper stands with the feet approximately shoulder-width apart, bent at the knees and waist, with the head up and the arms bent so that the forearms are almost parallel with the ground at hip-height. The palms are open in anticipation of catching the ball in an underhand scoop motion.

Style 1. While moving to receive a rolling ball, the goalkeeper places his or her body completely behind the ball with the feet only slightly apart (4 to 6 inches). The legs are kept straight, while the upper body bends forward at the waist. The arms are held out in front of the legs with palms facing up and open to receive the ball. The fingertips are almost touching the ground and the head is held so that the eyes can focus on the ball. As the ball makes contact with the fingers and palms, the ball is scooped and pulled to the chest.

INSTRUCTOR DEMONSTRATION

Your course instructor will demonstrate each recommended technique for style 1 for catching low balls. If you have questions, be sure to ask them before proceeding to the individualized task sequence. Refer to Photos 10.1A through C as your instructor explains and demonstrates each performance cue for this skill.

Photo 10.1A
Style 1, positioning

Photo 10.1B
Style 1, scooping

Photo 10.1C
Style 1, pulling to the chest

PERFORMANCE CUES

1. Place the body directly behind the intended path of the oncoming ball.
2. Keep the legs straight and no more than 4 to 6 inches apart.
3. Bend the upper body forward at the waist.
4. Open arms and palms to receive the ball.
5. On contact, scoop the ball and pull it to the chest.

READINESS DRILL

10-1. With one ball and a partner, stand 15 to 20 feet apart. Mark the distance with a cone on each end. Have your partner roll ground balls toward you to catch. Catch the ball using style 1 and then roll the ball back to your partner so that he or she can do the same. Each player should successfully complete 20 catches using style 1.

Style 2. While moving to receive a rolling ball, the goalkeeper places his or her right knee close to the ground (not touching) and within 4 to 6 inches of the left heel. The body is directly behind the path of the ball, and the upper body is bent at the waist and turned slightly in order to present a flat or square surface. The arms are held in front of the legs, the palms are open to receive the ball, and the head is so that the eyes can focus on the ball. As the ball makes contact with the fingers and palms, the ball is scooped and pulled to the chest. The goalkeeper may then stand up and consider how to initiate the attack.

INSTRUCTOR DEMONSTRATION

Your course instructor will demonstrate each recommended technique for style 2 for catching low balls. If you have questions, be sure to ask them before proceeding to the individualized task sequence. Refer to Photos 10.2A through C as your instructor explains and demonstrates each performance cue for this skill.

Photo 10.2A
Style 2, positioning

Photo 10.2B
Style 2, scooping

Photo 10.2C
Style 2, pulling to the chest

PERFORMANCE CUES

1. Place right knee close to the ground, 4 to 6 inches behind the heel of the front foot.
2. Right (trail) leg should be at 60 degrees to the path of the ball, making a wider protection.
3. Turn the upper body square to the ball and bend forward at the waist.
4. Open arms and palms to receive the ball.
5. Scoop and pull the ball to the chest on contact.

READINESS DRILL

10-2. With one ball and a partner, stand 15 to 20 feet apart. Mark the distance with a cone on each end. Have your partner roll ground balls toward you to catch. Catch the ball using style 2 and then roll the ball back to your partner so that he or she can do the same. Each player should successfully complete 20 catches using style 2.

If you experiencing difficulty with the readiness drills, refer to the **Performance Cues** and review each cue as it is presented. If you still have difficulty, ask your course instructor to assist you in applying these techniques.

Common Errors and Their Correction

Error	Correction
The knees are bent, causing the ball to strike them before it can be secured properly	Keep the legs as straight as possible.
The ball goes between your legs.	Keep legs no more than 4 to 6 inches apart.
Misplaying the ball after contact.	Watch the ball all the way into your hands.

CRITERION TASK 10-1

Partner-Checked

With one ball and a partner, stand 20 feet apart. Mark this distance with a cone at both ends. Have your partner kick medium-paced ground balls to you using an inside of the foot pass that forces you to move laterally 3 to 4 steps. You should catch each ball with style 1. Practice this task in blocks of 10 and record the number of successful catches for each block on the **Personal Recording Form**. When three individual block scores reach or exceed 7 out of 10, have your partner initial and date in the space provided. Then complete this task with style 2.

STYLE 1

Personal Recording Form									
Block 1	Block 2	Block 3	Block 4	Block 5	Block 6	Block 7	Block 8	Block 9	Block 10
___/10	___/10	___/10	___/10	___/10	___/10	___/10	___/10	___/10	___/10

Your partner's initials _____   Date completed _____

STYLE 2

Personal Recording Form									
Block 1	Block 2	Block 3	Block 4	Block 5	Block 6	Block 7	Block 8	Block 9	Block 10
___/10	___/10	___/10	___/10	___/10	___/10	___/10	___/10	___/10	___/10

Your partner's initials _____ Date completed _____

DEFENSIVE SKILL 2: CATCHING MEDIUM HIGH BALLS (BETWEEN KNEES AND CHEST)

This technique is adopted when the ball is approaching between the knee and the center of the chest. To catch a ball approaching at this height, the body must be behind the path of the oncoming ball. The goalkeeper stands with the feet approximately shoulder-width apart, and is bent at the knees and slightly forward at the waist. The head is up and the arms bent so that the forearms are almost parallel to the ground at hip-height. The palms are open in anticipation of catching the ball in an underhand fashion. You may prefer to have one foot slightly more forward than the other.

As the ball makes contact with the hands and forearms, they are triggered upward (scooping motion) to trap the ball against the chest where it can be held securely. The weight of the body, which is supported more on the front foot initially, is transferred more to the back foot on impact of the ball with the hands and arms. The body will also "give" somewhat in the mid-section to also help take some of the pace and force off the ball.

INSTRUCTOR DEMONSTRATION

Your course instructor will demonstrate each recommended technique for catching medium-high balls. If you have questions, be sure to ask them before proceeding to the individualized task sequence. Refer to Photos 10.3A and B as your instructor explains and demonstrates each performance cue for this skill.

Photo 10.3A
Positioning

Photo 10.3B
Trapping ball to chest

PERFORMANCE CUES

1. Place the body behind the path of the oncoming ball.
2. Place feet shoulder-width apart, with one foot slightly forward of the other.
3. Bend the upper body forward at the waist.
4. Outstretch arms with forearms parallel to the ground, elbows no more than body width apart, and palms open to receive the ball.
5. On impact of the ball, relax and "give" to absorb force of the ball.
6. Use hands and arms to scoop the ball and trap it to the chest.

READINESS DRILL

10-3. With one ball and a partner, stand 15 to 20 feet apart and toss the ball back and forth in an underhand fashion at a height between the knee and the center of the chest. Each player should successfully catch 20 medium-high balls.

If you experience difficulty with the readiness drill, refer to the **Performance Cues** and review each cue as it is presented. If you still have difficulty, ask your course instructor to assist you in applying these techniques.

Common Errors and Their Correction

Error	Correction
The ball is not caught cleanly.	Move quicker to get directly in front of the oncoming ball.
Ball bounces off chest.	Bring arms and hands up quickly to trap the ball better.
Swerving or spinning ball travels under your arm.	Keep elbows tight to the body.
Loss of balance while moving into position.	Shift weight from front foot to back foot.

CRITERION TASK 10-2

Partner-Checked

With a ball and a partner, stand 30 feet apart and mark both ends of this distance with a cone. You might choose to use a full-sized goal to catch balls that get by you. Have your partner kick medium-paced drive shots to you at a medium height (between your knees and chest) so that you have to move laterally 1 to 2 steps to catch the ball. Try to catch every shot, but if your partner's shot is not accurate, do not count that one if you are not successful. Practice this task in blocks of 10, recording the number of successful catches for each block on the **Personal Recording Form**. When three individual block scores reach or exceed 7 out of 10, have your partner initial and date in the space provided.

Personal Recording Form									
Block 1	Block 2	Block 3	Block 4	Block 5	Block 6	Block 7	Block 8	Block 9	Block 10
___/10	___/10	___/10	___/10	___/10	___/10	___/10	___/10	___/10	___/10

Your partner's initials _____ Date completed _____

DEFENSIVE SKILL 3: CATCHING HIGH BALLS
(BALLS HEAD-HIGH OR HIGHER)

Balls traveling toward the goal that are head high or higher present a diffi-cult challenge and a different set of circumstances to the goalkeeper. Most high balls are caught with the hands but will very often not have the body as a backup should the ball not be caught cleanly. Therefore, it is impor-tant to develop sound catching technique with the hands. The fingers are outspread with the thumbs almost touching. This is commonly called holding the hands in the W. The hands must be strong enough to with-stand the impact but soft enough to absorb the pace of the ball. The hands and arms will "give" on contact. Once the ball is caught, it is brought to the chest for safety.

The goalkeeper stands with the feet approximately shoulder-width apart and with one foot slightly ahead of the other. She or he is bent at the knees, with the head up and the arms bent so that the forearms and palms are fac-ing the field of play. The palms open and the fingers spread apart in antici-pation of catching the ball in the hands.

INSTRUCTOR DEMONSTRATION

Your course instructor will demonstrate each recommended technique for catching high balls. If you have questions, be sure to ask them before pro-ceeding to the individualized task sequence. Refer to Photos 10.4A through 10.4D as your instructor explains and demonstrates each performance cue for this skill.

PERFORMANCE CUES

1. Feet are shoulder-width apart with one foot slightly ahead of the other.
2. Arms are held up with the forearms and palms facing the field of play.
3. Hands are held closely together in a W with thumbs almost touching.
4. Hands and arms "give" on contact to absorb the force of the ball.

Photo 10.4A
Positioning

Photo 10.4B
Catch, rear view

Photo 10.4C
Catch, front view

Photo 10.4D
Pull to chest

READINESS DRILL

10-4. Get one ball and a partner. Mark off a distance of 20 feet and place a cone at each end. Have your partner toss the ball to you with an overhand throw to a point approximately head-high or slightly higher. Reaching upward you catch the ball in the W. After the ball has been safely brought to the chest, toss the ball in the same manner to your partner. Each player should complete 20 successful catches of high balls.

If you experience difficulty with the readiness drill, refer to the **Performance Cues** and review each carefully as it is presented. If you still have difficulty, ask your course instructor to assist you in applying these techniques.

Common Errors and Their Correction

Error	Correction
Ball goes through your hands.	Hold hands in W closer together with thumbs almost touching.
Ball bounces off your hands.	1. Hands and arms are held too stiffly. 2. Relax and "give" with the ball at contact.

CRITERION TASK 10-3

Partner-Checked

Get one ball and a partner. Mark off a distance of 20 feet and place a cone at each end. Have your partner throw high balls that require you to move 1 to 2 steps laterally to your left **and** must be fielded by jumping. Try to catch every toss, but if your partner's toss is not accurate, do not count that one if you are not successful. Practice this task in blocks of 10 and recording the number of successful catches for each block on the **Personal Recording Form**. When three individual block scores reach or exceed 7 out of 10, have your partner initial and date in the space provided. Repeat the task with tosses to your right side.

TOSSES TO THE LEFT

Personal Recording Form									
Block 1	Block 2	Block 3	Block 4	Block 5	Block 6	Block 7	Block 8	Block 9	Block 10
___/10	___/10	___/10	___/10	___/10	___/10	___/10	___/10	___/10	___/10

Your partner's initials _____ Date completed _____

TOSSES TO THE RIGHT

Personal Recording Form									
Block 1	Block 2	Block 3	Block 4	Block 5	Block 6	Block 7	Block 8	Block 9	Block 10
___/10	___/10	___/10	___/10	___/10	___/10	___/10	___/10	___/10	___/10

Your partner's initials _____   Date completed _____

BALLS THAT CAN'T BE CAUGHT

Many balls struck toward the goal are difficult if not impossible to catch by the goalkeeper. Decisions need to be made quickly as to whether a ball can be caught and possessed successfully. The goalkeeper's ultimate responsibility is to keep the ball from entering his or her team's goal. A catch and possession signal the beginning of an attack by the goalkeeper's team, but if the ball cannot be caught, a number of effective methods can be used to help prevent a goal from being scored. These methods are listed here as points of information and are not part of the instructional task sequence.

1. **Punching the ball.** Use one or both hands to strike the ball in a punching motion. This is done when there are players from each team in front of the goalkeeper and it is too risky to attempt to catch the ball. The intent is to clear the ball as far from the goal as possible and give the players and the goalkeeper time to recover.
2. **Deflecting, or parrying, the ball.** If only the fingertips or open hand can reach the ball, attempt to deflect the ball wide of the post or over the crossbar.
3. **Using the feet.** If the ball is played intentionally to the goalkeeper by a teammate, the goalkeeper must act like a field player and only use the feet to play the ball. Using the hands in this circumstance is against the rules. The intent is (1) to keep possession by playing the ball to a field player teammate or (2) to clear the ball out of a dangerous area. The goalkeeper

may also need to venture out of the penalty area to play a loose ball or to disrupt a breakaway. Once outside the penalty area, only the feet can be used to play the ball.

OFFENSIVE (ATTACKING) SKILLS

Once possession is gained by the goalkeeper, she or he can begin the attack toward the opponent's goal in a number of ways. There are two basic styles of attack. In the direct style the ball is played as far down the field as possible; in the indirect style the ball is played to a teammate, who will then systematically work the ball toward the opponent's goal by dribbling and passing to teammates. The method of getting the ball to a teammate from the goalkeeper is commonly referred to as *distributing* the ball. A goalkeeper invokes the direct style by punting or drop-kicking the ball from her or his own penalty area. The indirect style involves rolling or throwing the ball to a nearby teammate in or near the penalty area.

OFFENSIVE SKILL 1: ROLLING THE BALL TO A TEAMMATE (DISTRIBUTION)

The great advantage of this method lies in the fact that the ball quickly reaches a teammate who is in a position to control it easily and begin advancing it upfield. Once the goalkeeper possesses the ball, she or he identifies a teammate who is in a position to receive the ball. The player should be in an open space and not marked (covered) by a defender. This player must also indicate that she or he is ready and prepared to receive the ball by opening up to the ball (being able to see the goalkeeper and all other field players at the same time).

The goalkeeper uses an underhand motion to roll the ball to the feet of the receiving player. The goalkeeper's hand is spread wide under the ball and the gatekeeper steps toward the receiver with the foot opposite the throwing hand. The upper body leans forward at the waist. As the ball is released (bowling style), the goalkeeper's weight is transferred from the back foot to the front foot. Pace is important; if the roll is too hard, the ball will be difficult to receive; if too easy, the receiver loses valuable time in which to control and play the ball.

INSTRUCTOR DEMONSTRATION

Your course instructor will demonstrate each recommended technique for rolling the ball to an open teammate. If you have questions, be sure to ask them before proceeding to the individualized task sequence. Refer to Photo 10.5 as your instructor explains and demonstrates each performance cue for this skill.

PERFORMANCE CUES

1. Face the intended target (an open player).
2. Hold the throwing hand with fingers spread wide under the ball.
3. Use an underhand (bowling) motion.
4. Step with the foot opposite the throwing hand, and shift the weight from the back foot to the front foot.
5. Select an appropriate pace for the throw based on the distance to the receiver.

Photo 10.5
Rolling the ball

READINESS DRILL

10-5. Get one ball and a partner. Mark a distance of 20 yards and place a cone at each end. Simulate a medium or high catch and then roll the ball to your partner using the correct technique. Your partner receives the ball using the inside of the foot. Once under control, he or she then simulates a medium or high catch and then rolls the ball back to you; you also control it with the inside of the foot. A successful roll is one that does not cause the receiver to move more than 2 steps from his or her cone and that can be controlled easily. Bouncing rolls are not counted as successful. Each partner should complete 20 successful rolls in this drill.

If you experience difficulty with the readiness drill, refer to the **Performance Cues** and review each cue as it is presented. If you still have difficulty, ask your course instructor to assist you in applying these techniques.

Common Errors and Their Correction

Error	Correction
Inaccurate roll of the ball.	1. Hold the ball firmly in the palm of the hand with fingers spread wide for control.
	2. Step toward the intended target with the foot opposite the throwing hand.
Bouncing ball.	Bend forward at the waist and release the ball close to the ground.

CRITERION TASK 10-4

Partner-Checked

Get four or five balls and a partner. Mark off a distance of 20 yards and place a cone at each end. You can also use a full-sized goal at one end. If so, you should stand just in front of the goal with your partner at the marker cone. Your partner strikes the ball with the inside of the foot at a medium pace toward you, no more than 2 to 3 steps in either lateral direction. To count as a successful try, you must catch the ball, control it with your hands, and immediately roll the ball (distribute) to the feet of your partner, *no more than 2 steps from his or her cone*; The partner controls it with the inside part of the foot. Practice this task in blocks of 10 and record the number of successful attempts for each block on the **Personal Recording Form**. When three individual block scores reach or exceed 7 out of 10, have your partner initial and date in the space provided.

Personal Recording Form									
Block 1	Block 2	Block 3	Block 4	Block 5	Block 6	Block 7	Block 8	Block 9	Block 10
__/10	__/10	__/10	__/10	__/10	__/10	__/10	__/10	__/10	__/10

Your partner's initials _____   Date completed _____

OFFENSIVE SKILL 2: THROWING THE BALL (DISTRIBUTION)

A second distribution style involves throwing the ball to a teammate who is at a greater distance from the goalkeeper than can safely be rolled. A thrown ball can be used at a much greater distance, but it is often more difficult for the receiver to control than a rolling one. The choice of rolling or throwing the ball will most often depend on the specific situation at the time the ball is caught and must be distributed.

The ball is held with one hand and brought to a point approximately head high and slightly behind the body. The palm supports the ball from behind with the fingers spread wide for control. The goalkeeper's weight is on the back foot. The goalkeeper takes a step toward the intended target with the foot opposite the throwing hand. As the throw is made (baseball style), the weight shifts from the back foot to the front foot. The ball is thrown toward the feet of the player receiving the ball. This allows for quicker control by having the ball near the ground on arrival. The receiving player may need to utilize an upper-body trap to control the ball.

INSTRUCTOR DEMONSTRATION

Your course instructor will demonstrate each recommended technique for throwing the ball to an open teammate. If you have questions, be sure to ask them before proceeding to the individualized task sequence. Refer to Photo 10.6 as your instructor explains and demonstrates each performance cue for this skill.

PERFORMANCE CUES

1. Face the intended target.
2. Throw in an overhand motion (baseball style).
3. Step toward the target with the foot opposite that of the throwing hand.
4. Throw toward the receiver's feet to provide a better chance of controlling the ball quickly.
5. Shift the weight from the back foot to the front foot as the ball moves forward and you follow through.

Photo 10.6
Throwing the ball

READINESS DRILL

10-6. Get one ball and a partner. Mark a distance of 20 yards and place a cone at each end. Simulate a medium or high catch and then throw the ball to your partner using the correct technique. Your partner receives the ball using the inside of the foot, a thigh trap, or a chest trap. Once under control, he or she then simulates a medium or high catch and throws the ball back to you; you control it with one of the same three techniques. A successful throw is one that does not cause the receiver to move more than 2 steps from his or her cone and that can be controlled easily. Each partner should complete 20 successful throws in this drill.

If you experience difficulty with the readiness drill, refer to the **Performance Cues** and review each cue as it is presented. If you still have difficulty, ask your course instructor to assist you in applying these techniques.

Common Errors and Their Correction

Error

Not enough pace on the throw.

Correction

Hold the ball securely in the palm of the hand, with fingers spread wide, and throw the ball forcefully toward the receiver's feet.

Ball thrown off target.
Step directly toward the target with the foot opposite the throwing hand.

Ball is thrown too high.
Bend forward more at the waist, and direct the ball toward the receiver's feet.

CRITERION TASK 10-5

Partner-Checked

Get four or five balls and a partner. Mark off a distance of 20 yards and place a cone at each end. You can also use a full-sized goal at one end. If so, you should stand just in front of the goal with your partner at the marker cone. Your partner strikes the ball with the inside of the foot at a medium pace toward you, no more than 2 to 3 steps in either lateral direction. To count as a successful try, you must catch the ball, control it with your hands, and immediately throw the ball (distribute) to your partner, *no more than 2 steps from his or her cone*; the partner controls it with the inside part of the foot, a thigh trap, or a chest trap, no more then two steps from his/her cone. Practice this task in blocks of 10 and record the number of successful attempts for each block on the **Personal Recording Form**. When three individual block scores reach or exceed 7 out of 10, have your partner initial and date in the space provided.

Personal Recording Form									
Block 1	Block 2	Block 3	Block 4	Block 5	Block 6	Block 7	Block 8	Block 9	Block 10
___/10	___/10	___/10	___/10	___/10	___/10	___/10	___/10	___/10	___/10

Your partner's initials _____ Date completed _____

MODULE 11

MODIFIED SOCCER GAME

You have now learned all the basic skills needed to begin playing the game of soccer. This module will help you make the transition from drills to a modified game, stressing the various individual and complex skills presented in the preceding modules. The modified game will allow you many chances to use the skills learned in previous modules, using small-sided teams and a smaller playing field.

The game is structured as follows. It is played with seven players on a team (six field playes and a goalkeeper). The playing field should be approximately 70 yards long and 50 yards wide, with a full-sized goal on each end. Playing across half of a regulation college soccer field presents an excellent space for this version and two games can be conducted at the same time. Although full-sized goals are used, penalty areas can be modified slightly from the laws of the game. Field markings with paint or chalk are recommended but small cones can be used in place of lines.

Each team of seven players and a goalkeeper has the responsibility to attack and defend as a team. Possession of the ball is a key factor. When in possession, the strategy is to attack the opposing goal. When possession is lost, all players must defend to win back the ball. Positions of play are not as important as taking responsibility for attacking or defending based on where you are when the ball is won or lost. Some players will be more comfortable in a forward or midfield position, while others will be more comfortable in a more defensive role. Some players might like to play in the middle of the field while others might like to stay wide. Do not think in terms of assigned positions, except for each team's goalkeeper. Players should move around according to the flow of the game and the movement of the ball.

Do not be concerned with keeping score for this game. The purposes of this game are learning how to move to open spaces, how to pass and control the ball, defensive positioning, and goalkeeping. Be prepared for your instructor to stop the game when "teaching moments" occur, allowing him or her to provide feedback and comments to players as needed.

Play each game for 15 minutes. Assign a different person as goalkeeper for each game. You should play at least five games before you and your classmates progress to full-scale soccer games.

MODULE 12

MODIFIED RULES FOR PSIS SOCCER

READING ASSIGNMENT

Read the Modified Rules of Soccer presented in this module. If you have questions on any portion of the reading, be sure to ask you instructor for clarification or better yet, an example of that rule in action. Once you have completed the reading assignment, you can take the Soccer Knowledge Quiz at the end of this module.

The rules developed for this book are modified versions of the laws of the game. For a complete listing of the Laws of the Game, contact the Federation of International Football Associations, P.O. Box 85, 8030 Zurich, Switzerland, or the National Collegiate Athletic Association, Soccer Rules, 6201 College Boulevard, Overland Park, Kansas 66211-2422.

1. FIELD AND EQUIPMENT

A. FIELD OF PLAY

The normal field size for soccer is between 110 and 120 yards in length and 65 to 80 yards in width. For this course we propose a modified playing space of 65 to 75 yards long by 55 to 60 yards wide. This is for a game of seven players per team. Playing across one-half of a regulation-sized field provides an excellent space for the game outlined in Module 11. Penalty areas should be reduced to a space that is 15 yards out from the end line and 30 yards across. A halfway line should be marked across the designated space used for the seven versus seven game. For other small-sided games, the space should be reduced accordingly.

B. THE BALL

A regulation-sized soccer ball (size 5) is to be used for all participants in this course. A size 5 ball is between 27 and 28 inches in circumference and weighs approximately 15 ounces. It is recommended that a stitched ball rather than a rubber or synthetic laminated panel ball be utilized as it is much easier to control. An air pump should be available to keep proper air pressure in the ball during all practice and game sessions.

C. GOALS AND NETS

For small-sided games, it is recommended that small goals (approximately 4 feet high and 6 feet across) be utilized. Cones and/or flags can also be used to mark goal areas. For the shooting tasks, goalkeeper instruction, and some small-sided games (especially the seven versus seven game), full sized goals (8 feet high by 24 feet across) are recommended.

D. PLAYERS' EQUIPMENT

It is recommended that all players wear shin guards for safety. Soccer-type shoes are also recommended for the constant movement required in a 360-degree environment (starting, stopping, and changing directions). Cross-training shoes and turf shoes should work well. Shoes not designed for lateral movement and shoes with metal cleats should not be used. If you have any questions relative to appropriate footwear, contact your course instructor. Players should not wear anything that is dangerous to another player or to themselves (this includes jewelry). Clothing should be loose and designed for athletic purposes. Contrasting-color scrimmage vests should be provided to help designate team membership.

2. PLAYERS AND SUBSTITUTES

In this class, the emphasis is on learning the basic techniques and strategies for the game of soccer and to have an enjoyable experience. This is a cooperative venture and therefore everyone plays. Class size dictates the number of teams or groups and an even number of players on each team is not necessary. Team and group size are determined by where you are at a particular point in the course. Some participants in the class may progress faster through the units than you, and that is okay. The instructor will help regulate how the game structures evolve from class to class. A form of the game should be played every day at the end of class for a period of 10 to 15 minutes. This form may be one versus one, two versus two, or any other combination of players on a small field. Positions (defenders, midfielders, forwards, and goalkeepers) may be necessary once the game reaches seven versus seven but in small-sided games, all players serve as attackers and defenders based on who possesses the ball.

3. THE BALL IN AND OUT OF PLAY AND SCORING

The object of the game of soccer is to score goals. In most technical exercises in this book, scoring goals is an individual or small-group task. Modified rules have been developed to facilitate students learning the complex skills of playing the game.

A. THE START OF PLAY

There are a number of modified rules designed to help put the ball in play. To start a game or to restart after a goal, play is started with a *draw*. This is similar to a face-off in hockey, but the ball is already on the ground. A player from each team faces the ball with both feet on the ground. On the signal "draw", from the course instructor or student serving as a referee or observer, each player attempts to pull the ball backward to a teammate with the bottom of one foot. This allows for instant possession. Another modification allows the team who has been awarded the kickoff to kick the ball in any direction, including backward.

B. THE BALL IN AND OUT OF PLAY

Many small-sided game are conducted in a space delineated with cones or other markers. Lines are helpful but not necessary. If a ball clearly goes outside the playing space, it should be played back into the space by the team that did not cause it to go out of bounds. To put the ball back into play, it can be dribbled in, passed in with the feet, or thrown in. Players need to decide in advance which method they will utilize and know that it is okay to use all three if everyone agrees.

C. SCORING

A ball that goes completely into the goal (totally across the line) is considered to be a goal. If cones or flags are used to designate the goal, it must be determined in advance how high a ball can be struck and still count as a goal. Knee-high, the tops of the cone, or the tops of the flags are common designations.

4. VIOLATIONS AND MISCONDUCT

A. DIRECT KICKS

Any violent foul results in a direct free kick. Opponents must be 10 yards away from the ball when it is played. A direct kick can go directly into the goal without another person touching it. Direct kick fouls committed in your own penalty area result in a penalty kick from a spot 12 yards directly in front of the goal. Penalty kicks can only be defended by the goalkeeper. The following are examples of violations that allow direct kicks.

- Tripping or attempting to trip
- Pushing
- Holding
- Striking or attempting to strike
- Jumping at an opponent
- Kicking or attempting to kick
- Charging
- Using the knee on an opponent
- Fouling the goalkeeper who has possession of the ball
- Intentionally handling the ball

Committing any of these fouls during small-sided games is inappropriate, but there will be times when fouls will occur by accident. If violent-type fouls continually occur, something is wrong and your course instructor should intervene. If a violent foul or handball occurs during play, it will be up to the participants (especially the person who commits the foul or the person who is fouled) to enact the appropriate penalty (that is, a free kick).

B. INDIRECT KICKS

Violations that result in indirect kicks are typically illegal but nonviolent fouls. An indirect free kick permits a ball to be played freely with opponents 10 yards from the spot where it is played. An indirect kick must be touched by one other person (on either team) before it can legally be played into the goal. The following are examples of violations that result in indirect kicks.

- Playing the ball twice on restarts
- Unsportsmanlike conduct (searing or negative behavior)
- Dangerous play (playing the ball while in a dangerous position)
- Obstruction other than holding (impeding progress of a player to the ball)
- Offside (not having at least two opponents between you and the goal if you do not have the ball)
- Dissent (prolonged argument or disagreement)
- Goalkeeper interference (failure to allow the goalkeeper an opportunity to put the ball back into play)

• Illegal handling by the goalkeeper (if a field player intentionally plays a ball back to the goalkeeper, the goalkeeper may not use his or her hands to control it)

During modified or small-sided games, many of these rules will not come into play. Most small-sided games will not involve referees or goal-keepers. Monitoring players in an offside position is not necessary when play-ing small-sided games. Dangerous play and obstruction are the two most common rule violations that lead to an indirect free kick.

5. MODIFIED RULES FOR SMALL-SIDED GAMES

The game of soccer has many specific rules that govern play. A number of rules have been modified to facilitate play in the format of your PSIS soc-cer class. In all small-sided games leading up to seven versus seven, play-ers will serve as referees. If a foul or infraction occurs, "call it", put the ball down, and play it quickly. The instructor can also serve as an official, but the game is for the players and they should take on this responsibility. Recommendations for dealing with infractions of the rules during small-sided games follows:

A. HANDLING OF THE BALL

If a player intentionally handles the ball, it normally results in a direct free kick. In this format, a handball results in an indirect free kick from the spot of the foul.

B. OFFSIDE

If a player receives the ball in an offside position, it normally results in an indirect free kick by the opposing team from the spot of the infraction. In the small-sided game format, offsides will not be called in any of the game struc-tures.

C. PUTTING A BALL IN PLAY (Touchline)

If the ball goes out of play over the touchline during a small-sided game, the ball may be reentered in one of three ways: (1) the ball may be dribbled back into play, (2) the ball may be kicked (short or long pass), or (3) a regulation throw-in may be utilized. A member of the team that did not cause it to go out of bounds should put the ball back into play. The method should be agreed on prior to the start of the game and a regulation throw-in should be utilized in all seven versus seven games.

D. PUTTING A BALL IN PLAY (Endline)

If the ball goes over the endline during a small-sided game, a goal kick is taken from a point in front of the goal (within 3 yards). The goal kick is taken by the team defending the goal at the end where the ball goes out of play regardless of which team last touched it. In 7 vs. 7 games, corner kicks are taken if the defending team last touches the ball before it goes over the end-line.

E. EVERYONE PLAYS

Small-sided games are modified to allow everyone to play. The best method of learning the skills required to play soccer is to play the game. Create multiple teams and multiple games. Every game does not have to have an equal number of players. Substitutions can be utilized, but no player should be out of any game for more than 2 to 3 minutes.

F. FREE KICKS

All free kicks in small-sided games will be indirect. If a direct kick foul occurs in the penalty area (if one is utilized), a penalty kick by the person who is fouled can be taken.

E. COOPERATION

Every sport skill development class will have students who come to class with varied backgrounds. Some students have played a significant amount of time and may possess some very good skills, while others have little or no experience with any of the game skills or strategies. It is important for all students to work toward becoming better skilled players and to help each other reach this goal. The PSIS plan allows students to progress at their own rate of learning and stresses cooperation with a partner and within a small group to help facilitate learning to the fullest. By working together, the class will be much more enjoyable.

SOCCER KNOWLEDGE QUIZ

The soccer knowledge quiz is designed to assess your understanding of the basic skills, strategies, and rules involved in playing this team-oriented sport. The questions cover all 11 skill development modules in your PSIS soccer workbook. After you have studied each section of the book, completed the readiness tasks, criterion tasks, challenge tasks, and reviewed the modified rules of soccer, you are ready to contact your course instructor and request to take the soccer knowledge quiz.

You must score a minimum of 70% on the soccer knowledge quiz. (Your instructor may set the passing criterion at a different level, so be sure to check with him or her before taking the quiz.) If you not successful the first time, you should complete another review of the material and then request to take the quiz again during another class period.

Quiz score_____   Retest _____

Instructor's signature _____

Date completed _____

SOCCER KNOWLEDGE QUIZ

Name _____

Circle the letter of the correct answer to complete each statement.

1. The most effective method of mastering skill sequences in soccer is
   A.   practicing skills in a static environment
   B.   playing small-sided games
   C.   kicking back and forth with a partner
   D.   none of the above

2. For each person to learn soccer skills, everyone must work with a
   A.   partner
   B.   coach
   C.   ball
   D.   team

3. For each person to have the opportunity to become successful at playing soccer it is important
   A.   to practice static skills repetitively
   B.   to practice for hours and hours
   C.   practice with a partner
   D.   to practice in gamelike situations

4. Increased flexibility means more supple muscles which helps
   A.   reduce the risk of injury
   B.   learn soccer skills
   C.   learn soccer tactics and strategies
   D.   develop more power

5. When stretching, a target zone refers to
   A.   the number of muscle groups you need to stretch
   B.   the area of the muscle to be stretched
   C.   maximum tension in the muscle without pain
   D.   the time you spend stretching

6. The primary skill in ball possession is
   A.   receiving
   B.   dribbling
   C.   tackling
   D.   heading

7. Feinting is an action designed to
   A. score goals
   B. elude or deceive an opponent
   C. tackle the ball
   D. gain possession of the ball

8. The position of the nonkicking foot when making an inside of the foot pass should be
   A. directly behind the ball
   B. turned 90 degrees and locked
   C. next to the ball and pointed at the target

9. Striking the ball below the centerline will most likely result in
   A. the ball going to the left
   B. the ball going to the right
   C. the ball going high
   D. the ball hugging the ground

10. When receiving a ball that is rolling on the ground, it is important to
    A. relax the receiving foot on contact
    B. tense all muscles in the receiving foot
    C. move backward to receive the ball
    D. point the receiving foot toward the ball

11 When tackling the ball, the leg muscles should be
    A. relaxed
    B. tightened
    C. both

12. A challenge game introduces players to
    A. the game of soccer
    B. the rules of soccer
    C. the skills of soccer
    D. the tactics and strategies of playing soccer

13. The instep drive involves striking the ball with the
    A. shoelaces
    B. ankle
    C. inside of the foot
    D. toe

14. To keep an instep drive low, the upper body position should be
    A. leaning backward
    B. bent forward at the waist
    C. straight
    D. leaning in the direction you want the ball to go

15 The two most common upper body areas used to receive a ball are the
    A. head and chest
    B. thigh and chest
    C. stomach and chest
    D. stomach and thigh

16. When trapping a ball with the upper body, it is important to
    A. tighten the muscles of the head and neck
    B. relax and "give" with the ball
    C. bend forward at the waist
    D. close your eyes

17. In soccer, the head can be used to
    A. score goals
    B. clear balls out of danger
    C. pass to a teammate
    D. all of the above

18. When using a throw-in after an approach run, it is important to
    A. drag the toe of your front foot
    B. place both feet behind the endline
    C. throw the ball with the dominant arm
    D. start the ball from behind the head

19. The position of a goalkeeper's hands when catching a high ball must
    A. be shoulder-width apart
    B. have the forearms parallel with the ground
    C. be close together with thumbs almost touching
    D. none of the above

20. An example of a direct kick foul is
    A. offside
    B. obstruction
    C. unsportsmanlike behavior
    D. attempting to strike another player

Personal Progress Chart for PSIS Soccer

Module		1	2	3	4	5	6	7	8	9	10	11	12	13	14	15
12	Soccer Knowledge Quiz															
11	Modified Games															
10	Goalkeeping															
9	Throw-ins															
8	Heading															
7	Receiving with the Upper Body															
6	Instep Drive															
5	Kicking and Receiving															
4	Feinting															
3	Tackling															
2	Dribbling															
1	Stretching															
	Weeks in Class	1	2	3	4	5	6	7	8	9	10	11	12	13	14	15